THE

DAILY SPARK

180 easy-to-use lessons and class activities!

D0796010

THE DAILY SPARK

Critical Thinking
Journal Writing
Poetry
Pre-Algebra
SAT: English Test Prep
Shakespeare
Spelling & Grammar
U.S. History
Vocabulary
Writing

THE

DAILY SPARK

Spelling & Grammar

**SPARK
NOTES**

Copyright © 2004 by Spark Publishing

All rights reserved. No part of this book may be used or reproduced in any manner whatsoever without the written permission of the Publisher.

SPARKNOTES is a registered trademark of SparkNotes LLC

This edition published by Spark Publishing.

Spark Publishing
A Division of SparkNotes LLC
120 Fifth Avenue, 8th Floor
New York, NY 10011

ISBN 1-4114-0225-1

Please submit changes or report errors to *www.sparknotes.com/errors*.

Written by David Egan.

Printed and bound in the United States.

A Barnes & Noble Publication

Introduction

The *Daily Spark* series gives teachers an easy way to transform downtime into productive time. The 180 exercises—one for each day of the school year—will take students five to ten minutes to complete and can be used at the beginning of class, in the few moments before turning to a new subject, or at the end of class. A full answer key in the back of the book provides detailed explanations of each problem.

The exercises in this book may be photocopied and handed out to the class, projected as a transparency, or even read aloud. In addition to class time use, they can be assigned as homework exercises or extra credit problems.

The *Spelling & Grammar Daily Spark* covers spelling tactics, tricky grammar rules, and common mistakes. Instead of providing rote drills, the exercises give students fun, new ways to learn about spelling and grammar.

Spark your students' interest with the *Spelling & Grammar Daily Spark*!

Where in the Whirled?

In the next five minutes, brainstorm as many words as you can that contain the letters *w*, *h*, and *e*.

What is the longest word you came up with? How many words did you think of that contain *w*, *h*, and *e*, but don't begin with any of those three letters?

© 2004 SparkNotes LLC

There Are Plenty of *Ghoti* in the Sea

Did you know that the word *fish* can also be spelled "ghoti"? Well, why not? The *g-h* in *enough* is pronounced like an *f*, the *o* in *women* is pronounced like an *i*, and the *t-i* in *nation* is pronounced like *sh*.

Using similar reasoning, try to develop "alternative" spellings for the following words: *chest, mouse, care, lawn.*

DAILY SPARK SPELLING & GRAMMAR

© 2004 SparkNotes LLC

If Only Spelling Were More Simpul

Many words in the English language are spelled very differently from the way they're pronounced. For instance, the word *fuchsia* is pronounced "fyoosha."

Invent spellings for the following words that reflect the way they're actually pronounced: *choir, psycho, hymn, knight, myrrh.*

What do you think are the dictionary spellings for the words that are pronounced as the following: "skool," "skeem," "ruff," "lepurd," "skitsofrenia"?

© 2004 SparkNotes LLC

What's a Sentence Without Punctuation?

Did you know that punctuation doesn't just include commas, apostrophes, and periods, but it also covers the spaces between words and lowercase letters? Before punctuation was invented, texts were written in all caps without any spaces between words, making them hard to read. Rewrite the following paragraph using punctuation:

ITSVERYDIFFICULTTOREADSENTENCESWHENTHERESABSOLUTELYNO
PUNCTUATIONITMUSTHAVEBEENVERYDIFFICULTFORPEOPLETRYINGT
OREADBEFORETHEINVENTIONOFPUNCUTATIONDONTYOUTHINKBYIN
SERTINGSPACESPUNCTUTATIONMARKSANDLOWERCASELETTERSTHI
SPARAGRAPHWILLBECOMEMUCHEASIERTOREADWHATARELIEFTHAT
WILLBE

© 2004 SparkNotes LLC

DAILY SPARK SPELLING & GRAMMAR

© 2004 SparkNotes LLC

Snuffles Gets Active

The **active voice** occurs when the subject performs the action. In the **passive voice**, the subject of the sentence is acted on by another agent. Look at the following examples:

Passive voice: Snuffles was taken to the vet by my mom.
Active voice: My mom took Snuffles to the vet.

Eliminate the passive voice from your writing as much as possible. In the beginning, it will seem impossible, but after a while it will get easier, and you'll notice that your writing has become far more interesting and punchy.

Rewrite the following sentences, changing the passive voice to the active voice:

The exam was administered by the teacher.
Georgia's outfit was chosen by the saleswoman.
The city was invaded by barbarians.

Remember Mnemonics

A **mnemonic** is a device to help you remember something. Mnemonics are particularly useful when learning new vocabulary. For instance, it might be difficult to remember that *supercilious* means "arrogant," but it might help if you remind yourself that acting arrogant is "super silly."

Think of a word you have trouble remembering, and invent a mnemonic to help you.

© 2004 SparkNotes LLC

A Little Word Can Make a World of Difference

The word *not* is only three letters long, yet it can change the meaning of a sentence entirely. It's also a very slippery word that can fit into many different places in a sentence.

Where can the word *not* fit into the following sentence?

> John did tell Emily that there was enough sugar and salt but without making her feel bad.

Insert commas where needed in order to keep the sentence grammatically correct.

Watch Where You Put That Word!

Word order is crucial in determining the meaning of a sentence. *James hit Charles* is very different from *Charles hit James.*

See how many alternative sentences you can build using all the words in this sentence:

Rodrigo left Clara the keys and a note.

How does the meaning of the sentence change as you shift words around? Are some words easier to shift than others?

DAILY SPARK · SPELLING & GRAMMAR

© 2004 SparkNotes LLC

Are You a Quick Brown Fox or a Lazy Dog?

The following sentence contains all twenty-six letters of the alphabet:

The quick brown fox jumps over the lazy dog.

In the next five minutes, brainstorm as many sentences as you can that contain all twenty-six letters of the alphabet.

Love and Hate Are Just Three Steps Apart

You can change hate to love in just three steps—that is, you can change the word *hate* into the word *love* by changing one letter at a time, where each change produces a new word:

hate → *have* → *hove* → *love*.

See how many steps it takes you to make the following transformations: *dog* to *cat*, *jump* to *pool*, and *cool* to *warm*.

© 2004 SparkNotes LLC

Spelling in Alphabetical Order

The letters in the word *blow* are arranged in alphabetical order: *b* comes earliest in the alphabet, followed by *l*, followed by *o*, followed by *w*. The reverse is true for the letters in the word *wrong*.

See how many words you can think up whose letters are arranged either in alphabetical order or in reverse alphabetical order. What's the longest word you can come up with?

© 2004 SparkNotes LLC

The _____ Adjective

Adjectives are words that describe or modify another person or thing in the sentence. (The **articles** *a, an,* and *the* are also adjectives.) When used in moderation, adjectives can make your writing more vivid.

Fill in the blanks with an adjective:

The _____ acorn fell close to the _____ stoop, startling the _____ kid.

Without looking, the _____ dog raced across the _____ street, terrifying the _____ driver.

Twenty _____ children ran across the _____ playground, screaming _____ profanities.

© 2004 SparkNotes LLC

© 2004 SparkNotes LLC

Happily, Skittishly Approached

Adverbs (words like *quickly, grudgingly, slyly, completely*, and so on) describe or modify verbs, adjectives, and other adverbs.

See how many adverbs you can come up with to modify the verb *approached* in the following sentence. Try to include at least twenty adverbs in your list.

Lucy _____ approached the stranger.

What's in Your Name?

Notice that you can spell *dormitory* with exactly the same letters as *dirty room*. *Dirty room* is an **anagram** for *dormitory*.

See if you can find an anagram for your own name. Use just your first name, or use both your first name and last name if that's easier.

If you have a lot of trouble, try finding words using only, but not all, the letters in your name.

DAILY SPARK   SPELLING & GRAMMAR

© 2004 SparkNotes LLC

Adjectival Exchange

Write a paragraph with blanks where five adjectives should be. Make a list of five unrelated adjectives. Now exchange papers with a partner. Each person must fill in the blanks in the paragraph using the list of five adjectives.

Does your paragraph make grammatical sense? Does it make logical sense?

© 2004 SparkNotes LLC

Consecutive Class

The word *little* has two *t*'s in a row. The word *balloon* has two *l*'s in a row and two *o*'s in a row. Brainstorm as many words as you can that contain two sets of two letters in a row. Can you think of any words that contain three sets of two letters in a row?

DAILY SPARK SPELLING & GRAMMAR

© 2004 SparkNotes LLC

Making A Lot Out of A Little

Banana and *cocoon* are both six-letter words that contain only three letters. Think of as many words as you can that are at least three letters longer than the total number of letters in them.

What is the longest word you can think of in which no letter is repeated?

© 2004 SparkNotes LLC

Mouses and Hice

Mouse and *house* are similar nouns in the singular, but they follow different rules when they're made plural: *Mouse* becomes *mice*, and *house* becomes *houses*.

There's no good reason for this; it's just a quirk of English. *Mouse* could just as well become *mouses*, and *house* could just as well become *hice*. If that were the case, the sentence *Chase all of the mice out of the houses* would become *Chase all of the mouses out of the hice.*

List three other pairs of nouns that are similar in the singular, but which are made plural according to different rules.

© 2004 SparkNotes LLC

Rid and Hode

Ride and *hide* are similar verbs in the present tense, but they follow different rules when they're put in the past tense: *Ride* becomes *rode,* and *hide* becomes *hid.*

Again, this is just a quirk of English. *Ride* could just as well become *rid*, and *hide* could just as well become *hode.* If that were the case, the sentence *She rode into the forest and hid* would become *She rid into the forest and hode.*

List three other pairs of verbs that are similar in the present tense, but which follow different rules in the past tense.

Hello, Goodbye

Goodbye is a **contraction**, like *don't* or *isn't*. Originally, people parted by saying "God be with you," but over the years this phrase was shortened to *goodbye*.

List ten other contractions.

© 2004 SparkNotes LLC

e-Spelling

Spelling and grammar follow different conventions in different circumstances. For example, you're expected to use more formal English when writing an essay than you are when chatting with your friends. This doesn't mean that the English you use with your friends is "worse" than the English you use in essays. It's just that the context of an essay and the context of a casual conversation call for different conventions.

Email and instant messaging are governed by different conventions than those that govern books and papers. Many words are abbreviated—*thanks* can be spelled "tx," and *because* can be spelled "cuz." Many phrases are reduced to acronyms—*laughing out loud* becomes "lol," and *be right back* becomes "brb."

In the next five minutes, brainstorm as many spelling conventions as you can that are acceptable in online communication. Next to each one, write the "translation" in formal English.

e-Punctuation

Punctuation marks are used to convey tone and meaning that aren't conveyed by words alone. For example, a period signals the end of a thought, and an exclamation mark adds emphasis to what comes before it.

Over the past five or ten years, email and instant messaging have led to the invention of **emoticons**, which are similar to punctuation marks in their function. List as many as you can, and briefly define their meaning. Also, write a short sentence that includes a few emoticons.

© 2004 SparkNotes LLC

All in a Row

In the next five minutes, thinks of as many words as you can that have four or more consonants in a row or three or more vowels in a row.

What's the longest string of consonants in a single word that you can come up with? What's the longest string of vowels? Hint: there is one word in the English language that has six consonants in a row and one word that has five vowels in a row. These are both uncommon words, so don't worry if you can't think of them.

© 2004 SparkNotes LLC

Quite a Mouthful

In the next five minutes, try to think of: the longest one-syllable word you can, the longest two-syllable word you can, the shortest three-syllable word you can, and the shortest four-syllable word you can.

Were you able to find any one-syllable or two-syllable words that are longer than any four-syllable words?

© 2004 SparkNotes LLC

© 2004 SparkNotes LLC

Rhyme Crime

The rhyming parts of words are often spelled the same. For instance, *bore*, *chore*, and *core* all rhyme on the "ore" and are spelled the same. However, these three words also rhyme with the "oor" in *door* and the "or" in *for*.

In the next five minutes, brainstorm as large a group of rhyming words as you can, where the rhyming sound in each word is spelled differently.

To Influence the Result

People often mix up *effect* and *affect*. *Effect* is primarily a noun meaning "result," and *affect* is usually a verb meaning "to influence." Fill in the blanks with *affect* or *effect*:

The factory owner's huge donation did not _____ the senator's vote against the Clean Air Act.

Scientists are still determining the long-term _____s of smoking.

Scientists study how smoking _____s the lungs.

A cause-and-_____ relationship exists between exercise and weight loss.

The story of his childhood _____ed me deeply.

What _____ do you think George's arrival will have on Vera?

DAILY SPARK   SPELLING & GRAMMAR

© 2004 SparkNotes LLC

The Number Rule Amounts to This

Many people aren't quite sure when to use *amount* and when to use *number*. There's a pretty simple rule about when to use which: use *amount* with quantities that can't be counted and *number* with quantities that can be counted. For example:

The amount of time Isaac spent on this project is insane.
You wouldn't believe the number of hours Isaac spent on this project.

Shelly had a small amount of food on her plate.
Shelly had a small number of chips on her plate.

Write a paragraph describing the food you'd like to buy at the grocery store tonight. Use the words *amount* and *number* four times each.

© 2004 SparkNotes LLC

Apostrophe Plus *S*

To form the **possessive** of most singular nouns, simply add an **apostrophe** (') and an *s* to the end of the word. For example, *cat* becomes *cat's*, *John* becomes *John's*, and *math teacher* becomes *math teacher's*.

Simplify the following five sentences by turning phrases into possessive nouns where possible:

The bike of the boy cost twenty bucks.

The dog of Jenny ran away yesterday.

The speech of that woman made me sleepy.

The left leg of that horse hurts.

The umbrella of Gwendolyn broke in the strong winds.

DAILY SPARK   SPELLING & GRAMMAR

© 2004 SparkNotes LLC

Doubling Consonants

Some pairs of consonants often occur together, such as *st* and *th*. Other pairs of consonants occur together only very rarely, such as the *mq* in *kumquat*.

Brainstorm as many consonant pairs as you can. For each, provide an example of a word in which the pair occurs.

© 2004 SparkNotes LLC

Doubling Vowels

Some pairs of vowels often occur together, such as *ee* or *ai*. Other pairs of vowels occur together only rarely, such as the *uo* in *quote*.

In the next five minutes, brainstorm as many vowel pairs as you can. For each, provide an example of a word in which the pair occurs. With the exception of *ii* and *uu*, you should be able to find an example of every possible pairing of the five vowels *a*, *e*, *i*, *o*, and *u*.

DAILY SPARK SPELLING & GRAMMAR

© 2004 SparkNotes LLC

Missing Sounds

Compose the longest sentence you can that doesn't contain the letter *e*.

Compose the longest sentence you can that doesn't contain the letter *a*.

Which of these two letters did you find it was harder to do without?

© 2004 SparkNotes LLC

Missing Halves

Compose the longest sentence you can using only letters from the first half of the alphabet—that is, the letters *a* through *m*. If you're having trouble, you may also use *s* and *t*.

Compose the longest sentence you can using only letters from the second half of the alphabet—that is, the letters *n* through *z*. Add *a* and *e* if you're having trouble.

DAILY SPARK SPELLING & GRAMMAR

© 2004 SparkNotes LLC

Scrabble® Names

The popular board game Scrabble® assigns different point values to different letters depending on how commonly they occur in words. The point system is as follows:

1 point: *a, e, i, l, n, o, r, s, t, u*
2 points: *d, g*
3 points: *b, c, f, m, p*
4 points: *h, v, w, y*
5 points: *k*
8 points: *j, x*
10 points: *q, z*

Calculate how many points you would get for spelling your own name.

Think of as many words as you can that have the same point value as your name.

© 2004 SparkNotes LLC

Same Old Rule

To make singular nouns ending in *s* **possessive**, add an **apostrophe** (') and an *s* to the end of the word, just as you would with a word ending in *w* or *t* or any other letter. For example, *grass* becomes *grass's*, *mantis* becomes *mantis's*, and *glass* becomes *glass's*.

Write a paragraph about a dress. Using apostrophes, describe six of the dress's features.

DAILY SPARK · SPELLING & GRAMMAR

© 2004 SparkNotes LLC

The Photographs' Rabbits' Doctors

Most plural nouns end in *s*. To make these nouns **possessive**, simply add an **apostrophe** (') to the end of the word. For example, *photographs* becomes *photographs'*, *rabbits* becomes *rabbits'*, and *doctors* becomes *doctors'*.

Add apostrophes to the following sentences where they are needed:

The students voices filled the auditorium.
The lawyers fees exceeded two million dollars.
The dogs barking kept me up all night.
The soldiers parents worried about their children.

Now write four sentences of your own using possessive plural nouns.

© 2004 SparkNotes LLC

Dickens, Euripides, Descartes

Just when you thought you had apostrophes figured out, along comes the slightly tricky rule for making proper nouns ending in *s* **possessive**. In most cases, simply add an **apostrophe** (') and an *s* to these nouns, as you would with any other noun. For example, *Dickens* becomes *Dickens's*.

But if the last syllable of the noun ends in an "eez" sound, add only an apostrophe: *Euripides* becomes *Euripides'*. If the *s* at the end of the noun is unpronounced, also add only an apostrophe: *Descartes* becomes *Descartes'*.

Practice these rules on the following phrases:

The architecture of Athens

The motorcycle of James

The movies of Bette Davis

© 2004 SparkNotes LLC

It's Not at Its Best

Write two sentences, one that contains *he's* and *his* and the other that contains *she's* and *her*.

Now substitute *it's* and *its* into the two sentences. Which words are replaced by *it's* and which are replaced by *its*? If you're not sure, try writing *it is* instead of *it's*.

© 2004 SparkNotes LLC

Who's Bad?

Badly is an adverb used to describe how something is done. *Bad* is an adjective that refers to health or feelings. *Bad* is also used to complete linking verbs, such as *seem, look, taste,* and *smell.*

Fill in the blanks with *bad* or *badly*:

I feel _____ that Harriet wasn't invited.

Rudolph dances _____, but at least he tries hard.

The soup tasted _____ on the first day and even worse on the second.

You look really _____. When was the last time you slept?

Ms. Kramer spells_____, so it's lucky she has a smart secretary.

Roger wanted to see Gisele so _____ that he postponed his flight.

© 2004 SparkNotes LLC

Smart, Smarter, Smartest

Most regular adjectives (like *smart*) can be modified by adding *-er* (*smarter*) or *-est* (*smartest*), depending on the degree of the comparison. Unmodified adjectives are in the **positive degree**, adjectives with the *-er* ending are in the **comparative degree**, and adjectives with the *-est* ending are in the **superlative degree**. For example, *Many late-night comedians are funny* (positive degree). *David Letterman is funnier* (comparative degree) *than Jay Leno, but Jon Stewart is the funniest* (superlative degree) *of all.*

Write a paragraph comparing members of your family. Use comparative and superlative forms of all the following adjectives, as well as any others that pop into your head: *pretty, kind, smart, mean, old.*

© 2004 SparkNotes LLC

You're a Terrible Parent!

You're is the contraction of *you are* (*You're coming tonight, aren't you?*). *Your* is a possessive pronoun (*Are you bringing your brother?*). If you're not sure which is correct, try substituting *you are*. If that sounds wrong, you know you should use *your* instead.

Fill in the blanks with *you're* or *your*:

_____ son has a serious behavior problem, probably because _____ much too indulgent with him. _____ child-rearing methods are too relaxed. _____ making a mistake if you think _____ devil-may-care approach to parenting will work. _____ son doesn't respect you, and if this lack of discipline continues, _____ going to wind up bailing him out of jail one day.

© 2004 SparkNotes LLC

Running Through the Alphabet

Write a short story that contains twenty-six sentences, where the first word of the first sentence begins with the letter *a*, the first word of the second sentence begins with the letter *b*, and so on. Feel free to use a dictionary if you need help, especially when you reach the letter *x*!

© 2004 SparkNotes LLC

Free Ice Cream for Everyone!

The **conditional** is the verb form used to describe something uncertain, something that's conditional or dependent upon something else. The conditional formula is *If . . . were . . . would.* For example, *If I were president, I would give everyone free ice cream.* Note that it is incorrect to write *If I was president, I would give everyone free ice cream.*

Write five sentences that use the conditional correctly.

© 2004 SparkNotes LLC

Rolling Out the Square Metaphors

A **metaphor** is a comparison of a thing, person, or idea in terms of another. Metaphors don't use the words *like* or *as*. For example, *Dave is a pig* is a metaphor.

Metaphors are supposed to make our meaning clearer to others, but sometimes metaphors are misused in a way that confuses meaning. For example, a recent travel guide described a wealthy businessman's financial empire as having tentacles in tourism, entertainment, and transport. It explained that this empire had recently collapsed, leaving mountains of debt and fraud investigations in its wake. By its use of metaphor, this description asks us to imagine an empire that has tentacles, which then collapses, leaving mountains in its wake, as if it's a ship. When metaphors create such a confused message they are called **mixed metaphors**.

Write a soppy love letter using as many mixed metaphors as possible.

A Variety of Sentences

Five common parts of speech are the verb, the adverb, the adjective, the noun, and the preposition. Write a few sentences that use all of these parts of speech.

© 2004 SparkNotes LLC

After School, I Use Coordinating Conjunctions

Coordinating conjunctions—*and, but, for, or, nor, so, yet*—help join two independent clauses together. For example, *William begged for months, and finally his mother relented.*

Write a paragraph about what you usually do after school. Use as many coordinating conjunctions as possible.

The Fragment Only Millionaires Can Fix

Sentence fragments have a subject but lack a correctly conjugated verb. Fragments can be difficult to recognize, in part because they are so common in advertising. *The sports car only millionaires can afford* is an example: *only millionaires can afford* is actually an adjectival phrase modifying the subject *sports car*. A corrected version of this sentence might read, *The sports car only millionaires can afford has its lights on.*

Use this trick to check whether you have a fragment on your hands: rephrase your sentence as a yes-or-no question. If it doesn't make sense, it's a fragment. For example, *Was the sports car only millionaires can afford?* makes no sense, but *Does the sports car only millionaires can afford have its lights on?* does make sense.

Come up with four sentence fragments, and then turn them into complete sentences.

© 2004 SparkNotes LLC

© 2004 SparkNotes LLC

The Red Redness Redly Reddenned

The word *short* is an adjective, but it can also be expressed as a noun (*shortness*), an adverb (*shortly*), and a verb (*shorten*). Other adjectives cannot be expressed as a noun, adverb, and verb. For example, *nice* can be expressed as a noun (*nicety*) and an adverb (*nicely*), but there is no verb for *nice*.

Think of five adjectives that don't have a corresponding noun, adverb, or verb. For each adjective, invent the missing noun, adverb, or verb.

Similar Similes

A **simile** is a comparison using *like* or *as*, as in *my heart is like cellophane*.

Think of several words or phrases to complete this simile: My heart is like . . .

© 2004 SparkNotes LLC

Mismatched Similes

Come up with a word or phrase to complete each of the following similes:

I'm as hungry as . . .
My hair is like . . .
A rainy day is like . . .
The cars on the street sound like . . .
I woke up feeling like . . .

Now mismatch the words or phrases you came up with, applying them to the other four similes. What sorts of results do you come up with? Do any of the similes make sense when they're mismatched?

© 2004 SparkNotes LLC

Fill in the Blank

Take the following sentence:

The driver lost control of the car, and it slid off the road and into a lamppost.

Try to substitute as many metaphors as you can for the words in this sentence, while ensuring that someone reading the sentence could still understand it clearly. (If you were doing this to the sentence *He played the piano*, for example, you might write *He tickled the ivories*.)

© 2004 SparkNotes LLC

No, You're the Oxymoron

An **oxymoron** is a contradiction in terms, like *old news* or *loose tights*.

In the next five minutes, think of as many oxymorons as you can.

© 2004 SparkNotes LLC

Running On and On

A **run-on** (or **fused**) **sentence** consists of two independent clauses joined together without punctuation. For instance, *We dashed across the street at top speed we didn't want to get hit by a car* is a run-on sentence. An extremely long sentence is *not* necessarily a run-on sentence.

What's the longest sentence you've ever written? Ten words? Twenty? Write the longest sentence you can without creating a run-on. If you're up to the challenge, try writing a fifty-word sentence. Believe it or not, it can be done!

SPELLING & GRAMMAR

© 2004 SparkNotes LLC

The Fix Is In

Comma splices occur when a comma is used to join two independent clauses. There are two easy ways to fix comma splices like this one: *He loved reruns, she preferred reality shows.*

    1. Insert a **coordinating conjunction** (*and, but, for, or, nor, so, yet*) before the comma. For example, *He loved reruns, but she preferred reality shows.*

    2. Connect the two independent clauses with a **semicolon**. For example, *He loved reruns; she preferred reality shows.*

Come up with three comma splices, and then offer two corrections for each.

© 2004 SparkNotes LLC

A caPtL IDa

The following words have been written using a new rule of spelling: *hLO, TchR, spLEng, mXEcO, haPnS, crAZ.*

What are the six words spelled above? What is the spelling rule that has been applied to them?

Use the same spelling rule to spell the following words: *peculiar, behavior, express, enticing, sentinel, caterer.*

© 2004 SparkNotes LLC

The Difference a Few Dots Can Make

Punctuation may seem like a small thing, but it can radically alter the meaning of a sentence. For example, consider the difference between these two signs:

Private. No swimming allowed.
Private? No. Swimming allowed.

The words remain the same, but a change in punctuation gives them opposite meanings. Find new ways to punctuate the following sentences so as to give them a different meaning:

I'm sorry you can't come with us.
The butler stood by the door and called the guests' names.
Look at that man eating chicken.
A smart dog knows its master.
Call me "fool" if you want.

© 2004 SparkNotes LLC

Ica n'tqu itefo ll owyou

The following short paragraph has spaces inserted in all the wrong places. Rewrite the paragraph so that it makes sense.

T hespa ceswep utbet we enw ordsa rees sent ia lforma kings ens eofwh atwer ead. Wit houtt he sespa ces, ourwo rdsbe co meaninc omprehe nsi bleju mble. Witha llthes pac esi nth ewron gp laces, or dina rywr itin gsta rtstolo oklik esom et hin gwrit teni naf ore ignlan gua ge.

© 2004 SparkNotes LLC

As She Patted the Dog's Head . . .

Suppose you want to quote parts of the following sentence from Charlotte Brontë's *Jane Eyre*: *"As she patted the dog's head, bending with native grace before his young and austere master, I saw a glow rise to that master's face."*

To indicate omitted material from the beginning or middle of a quotation, use **ellipses**:

"As she patted the dog's head . . . I saw a glow rise to that master's face."

To omit words from the end of a sentence, indicate the omission with ellipses, and then indicate the end of the sentence with a period: *"As she patted the dog's head, bending with native grace before his young and austere master . . . ."*

Rewrite the following sentences from *Jane Eyre* five times, omitting different parts each time:

"He ran headlong at me: I felt him grasp my hair and my shoulder: he had closed with a desperate thing. I really saw in him a tyrant, a murderer."

© 2004 SparkNotes LLC

Exclamation Points!!!!!!

Exclamation points, which signal strong emotion, should be used only when absolutely necessary.

Write a paragraph about the most exciting thing that has ever happened to you, and fill it with exclamation points. When you're done, rewrite it, changing every exclamation point to a period. Which version do you prefer? Why?

© 2004 SparkNotes LLC

© 2004 SparkNotes LLC

Headline Blues

Newspaper editors work under intense pressure and must write up news headlines very quickly. Occasionally, the headlines turn out to mean something very different than what they were intended to mean.

Each of the following headlines actually appeared in a newspaper at some point. For each one, write out two full sentences, the first expressing what you think the headline was supposed to mean, and the second expressing the alternative meaning that you could draw from the headline.

DRUNK GETS NINE MONTHS IN VIOLIN CASE
FARMER BILL DIES IN HOUSE
IRAQI HEAD SEEKS ARMS
BRITISH LEFT WAFFLES ON FALKLAND ISLANDS
MINERS REFUSE TO WORK AFTER DEATH
KILLER SENTENCED TO DIE FOR SECOND TIME IN TEN YEARS

MA-DE in the USA

All fifty U.S. states and ten Canadian provinces, as well as all U.S. possessions and Canadian territories, have a two-letter code that can be used for mailing purposes. Try to form words by combining these two-letter codes into words of four, six, eight, or more letters.

The two-letter codes are as follows:

United States codes: **AL, AK, AR, AS, AZ, CA, CO, CT, DE, DC, FL, GA, GU, HI, IA, ID, IL, IN, KS, KY, LA, MA, MD, ME, MI, MN, MO, MP, MS, MT, NC, ND, NE, NH, NJ, NM, NS, NV, NY, OH, OK, OR, PA, PR, RI, SC, SD, TN, TX, UT, VA, VI, VT, WA, WI, WV, WY**

Canadian codes: **AB, BC, MB, NB, NL, NS, NT, NU, ON, PE, QC, SK, YU**

© 2004 SparkNotes LLC

Periodic F-U-N

The periodic table is an essential tool in chemistry. It can also be used to form all sorts of words. Every element in the periodic table is characterized by a one- or two-letter symbol. Form as many words as you can by combining symbols in the periodic table.

Some symbols in the periodic table are as follows:

Ac, Ag, Al, Am, Ar, As, At, Au, B, Ba, Be, Bh, Bi, Bk, Br, C, Ca, Cd, Ce, Cf, Cl, Cm, Co, Cr, Cs, Cu, Db, Ds, Dy, Er, Es, Eu, F, Fe, Fm, Fr, Ga, Gd, Ge, H, Ha, He, Hf, Hg, Ho, Hs, I, In, Ir, K, Kr, La, Li, Lr, Lu, Md, Mg, Mn, Mo, Mt, N, Na, Nb, Nd, Ne, Ni, No, Np, O, Os, P, Pa, Pb, Pd, Pm, Po, Pr, Pt, Pu, Ra, Rb, Re, Rf, Rh, Rn, Ru, S, Sb, Sc, Se, Sg, Si, Sm, Sn, Sr, Ta, Tb, Tc, Te, Th, Ti, Tl, Tm, U, V, W, Xe, Y, Yb, Zn, Zr

Jus' Rollin' Along

An **apostrophe** (') is a marker to show that letters have been left out. For example, the apostrophe in *don't* shows that the *o* in *not* is missing.

In everyday speech, we rarely pronounce all the letters that would be written out if we were writing in formal English. Not only do we shorten phrases like *did not* to *didn't* and *I am* to *I'm*, but we also shorten other words whose abbreviated spellings are not commonly found in writing—for example, most people say *prob'ly* or even *pro'ly* instead of *probably*.

Write down four other words that we abbreviate when we're speaking.

© 2004 SparkNotes LLC

Weird Science

You may be familiar with the spelling rule *"i* before *e*, except after *c"*—that is, when writing words where an *i* and an *e* appear together, we put the *i* first, as in *belief* or *sieve*, except after the letter *c*, when *e* comes first, as in *conceited* or *receive*.

Think of as many words as you can that are an exception to this rule. See if there are any patterns in the exceptions you find. Can you formulate any sub-rules that take account of these exceptions?

© 2004 SparkNotes LLC

A to Z, First and Last

DAILY SPARK

SPELLING & GRAMMAR

© 2004 SparkNotes LLC

Come up with twenty-five words. The catch? The twenty-five words should start with the letters *a* through *z* and end with the letters *a* through *z*, and no two words should start with the same letter and no two words should end with the same letter. (There are no familiar English words that end with the letter *q*, which is why you're asked for twenty-five instead of twenty-six.)

Hint: Try eliminating difficult letters like *x* and *j* first, while saving easier letters like *e* and *r* until you really need them.

Not Feeling Too Good Myself

Good is an adjective, not to be confused with *well*, which is an adverb.

Fill in the blanks with *good* or *well*:

Theo played _____ in the ballgame.

The pie tasted _____ last night.

Quentin did a _____ job redecorating.

I don't feel _____ today.

I wish I could sing as _____ as William.

© 2004 SparkNotes LLC

Old Dealer or Old Cars?

Hyphens are used to make **compound words** like *daughter-in-law, master-at-arms, six-pack, mass-produce, higher-up,* and *go-between.* Hyphens also help form **compound modifiers** (two or more words that express a single concept) like *six-year-old child* and *two-thirds majority.*

Hyphens can change the meaning of a phrase. *Old car dealer,* for example, means something very different from *old-car dealer.*

Write three sentences featuring compound words, and three more featuring compound modifiers.

© 2004 SparkNotes LLC

DAILY SPARK

SPELLING & GRAMMAR

© 2004 SparkNotes LLC

Fashion Union

In the next five minutes, think of words that end with the letters *ion*.

Once you have your list, classify these words into different categories according to how the words are spelled or pronounced.

They're All There with Their Friends

Homonyms are words that are pronounced in the same way. For example, *sea* and *see* are homonyms.

Think of as many homonyms as you can. For each set, compose a sentence in which both homonyms appear.

DAILY SPARK SPELLING & GRAMMAR

© 2004 SparkNotes LLC

DAILY SPARK SPELLING & GRAMMAR

© 2004 SparkNotes LLC

Double Trouble

Start going through the alphabet, and for each letter try to come up with a word in which that letter is doubled. (For instance, when you get to *b*, you might think of *babble*.)

Dreaded Exercise

Come up with as many words as you can in which the first letter of the word is the same as the last letter of the word.

DAILY SPARK SPELLING & GRAMMAR

© 2004 SparkNotes LLC

Mission Diacritical

In each of the following sentences, the spelling of words has been altered somewhat according to a certain rule. Try to work out what the rule is in each case, and then spell the sentence as you normally would:

{T}ey have {t}ou{g}t about getting {t}eir flu {s}ots before lun{c}.

The bêt mûician hâ only hî innate talents and a little luck.

The bett! they p!form, the mo! the sing!'s voice will rev!b!ate.

The 6enius of the ma6ic show 9ot the 9uests up on their feet, applauding in deli3ht.

Thye lingered over thier haerty mael for an huor.

© 2004 SparkNotes LLC

Numerical Inflation

The late comedian Victor Borge suggested that just as inflation causes prices to rise over time, so it should cause the numbers in language to rise over time. He proposed we add one to every number that appears in language so that, for instance, *tooth* becomes *threeth*.

Using the principle of language inflation, add one to every "number" that appears in the following sentences and then rewrite the sentences:

For once, you should interrogate someone using only the formal techniques.

Do you want people to be tender and benign, or do you prefer asinine people?

I often wear a tutu, and I wonder why no one thinks it's great.

The canine's mate showed great fortitude during the tense wait.

The debate over forensics wasn't conducted with exactitude.

© 2004 SparkNotes LLC

On the Opposite Side

The **antonym** of a word is the word that means the exact opposite. For example, *good* and *bad* are antonyms.

In the following sentences, find an antonym for each of the underlined words. Then rewrite the sentences using the antonyms.

When the <u>white</u> light <u>shines</u>, I <u>close</u> my eyes.

<u>Last</u> year, the army <u>advanced</u> as <u>far</u> as the <u>beautiful</u> <u>hills</u>.

<u>After</u> <u>trudging</u> <u>toward</u> the <u>tunnel</u>, they <u>succeeded</u> in <u>gaining</u> a <u>clear</u> <u>advantage</u>.

Her <u>newfound</u> <u>passion</u> for <u>life</u> was <u>sadly</u> <u>temporary</u>.

<u>On</u> <u>top</u> of the <u>mound</u>, she <u>lifted</u> her hand in <u>defiance</u>.

I *Adore* Italics

Italics or **underlining** are used for movie and book titles, foreign words not commonly used in English, and emphasis. (Be sure to choose either italics or underlining and stay consistent throughout an entire document.)

Indicate which words should be italicized (or underlined) in the following sentences:

I am so furious at you!

Janet loves The Lord of the Rings.

Their apartment has really nice gemutlichkeit.

© 2004 SparkNotes LLC

DAILY SPARK   SPELLING & GRAMMAR

Romulus and Rebus

A **rebus** is a word puzzle that represents words pictorially. For example, "mUs" is a rebus for *ambiguous* (M, big U, S). Try to solve the following rebuses:

```
M   E
A   L
```

STA4NCE

```
FUNNY FUNNY
WORDS WORDS
WORDS WORDS
```

M1Y L1I1F1E

HOROBOD

It's All Prefixed Up

DAILY SPARK SPELLING & GRAMMAR

A **prefix** is a string of letters that can be attached to the beginning of a word to alter its meaning. For example, the prefix *pre-* means "before." If we want to talk about something that occurs at an earlier date than something else, we say it *predates* it. You might also have noticed that the word *prefix* itself contains the prefix *pre-*: *prefix* means strings of letters we *fix* before other words.

In the left-hand column, below, are a number of prefixes. In the right-hand column are a number of word roots. See how many different words you can form by attaching prefixes to word roots.

re	*hale*
sub	*fluence*
ex	*sist*
in	*lieve*
con	*tain*
be	*ordinate*

© 2004 SparkNotes LLC

It's All Suffixed in Place

A **suffix** is a string of letters that can be attached to the end of a word to alter its meaning or change it to a different part of speech. For example, the suffix *-less* means "without," so a person without help can be called *helpless*. The suffix *-ful* is a common way of turning a noun into an adjective. *Beauty* or *wonder* can become *beautiful* or *wonderful*.

In the left-hand column, below, are a number of word roots. In the right-hand column are a number of suffixes. See how many different words you can form by attaching word roots to suffixes.

govern	*er/or*
up	*ment*
contain	*ward*
back	*ly*
kind	*ness*
valid	*ity*

© 2004 SparkNotes LLC

One of the Less Tricky Rules

Some people aren't sure when to use *fewer* and when to use *less*. Here's the rule: Use *fewer* when talking about something that can be counted (such as hours, dollars, and animals); use *less* when talking about something that can't be counted (such as time, money, and space).

Write six sentences about your classes, three that use *less* and three that use *fewer*.

DAILY SPARK   SPELLING & GRAMMAR

© 2004 SparkNotes LLC

Compounded Together

A **compound word** is a word that puts two smaller words together. For example, *blackboard* is a compound of *black* and *board*.

Think of five objects, activities, or ideas you're familiar with, and invent a compound words that describes each one accurately.

© 2004 SparkNotes LLC

Nine Nice Nights

Take a few minutes and brainstorm as many words as possible that contain the sound "ine" as in *nine*. Then brainstorm as many words as possible that contain the sound "ice" as in *nice*. After that, brainstorm as many words as possible that contain the sound "ite" as in *night*.

Which of these three sounds was easiest to find words for?

© 2004 SparkNotes LLC

Unusual Sentences

See if you can come up with at least one example of each of the following:

A sentence that contains no nouns.

A sentence that contains three adverbs, one of which modifies a verb and one of which modifies an adjective.

A sentence that contains four adjectives, three adverbs, two nouns, and one verb.

A sentence that contains a noun, adjective, adverb, and verb, but nothing else (no conjunctions, no articles, no prepositions, etc.).

It's Not That Hard

Almost everyone gets *its* and *it's* confused, and it's easy to see why: usually, when we want to show **possession**, we use an **apostrophe** (') and an *s* (*Mara's attitude, the dog's breakfast,* and so on). For this reason, people often use *it's* when they want to show possession. Unfortunately, that is wrong, wrong, wrong. *It's* is a **contraction** of *it is*; *its* is the word that shows possession.

Fill in the blanks with *it's* or *its*:

_____ all right, _____ okay, you'll be working for us someday.

The storm unleashed _____ fury right above our house.

When all's said and done, _____ better to be the one who ends the relationship.

The cat meowed _____ head off, as if to say, "_____ time for my dinner!"

© 2004 SparkNotes LLC

Now I Lay Me Down to Sleep

Lie, lay—who can tell the difference? You can, if you memorize this:

You *lie* down for a nap.
Yesterday, you *lay* down for a nap.
You *lay* something down on the table.

Write six sentences that use *lie* and *lay* correctly.

I Feel Like That's Right

In formal writing, avoid using *like* as a **conjunction** (a word that joins two parts of a sentence). We're all prone to writing *I feel like he's angry at me* or *She shops like it's going out of style*. But these constructions are not technically right. Corrected, these sentences would read *I feel as if he's angry at me* and *She shops as if it's going out of style*.

Come up with six sentences that use *as if* correctly.

DAILY SPARK SPELLING & GRAMMAR

© 2004 SparkNotes LLC

A Bellwether for *Whether* and *Weather*

When do you use the word *whether* and when do you use the word *weather*?

Fill in the blanks with *whether* or *weather*:

_____ the _____ is cold, or _____ the _____ is hot, we'll be together
whatever the _____, _____ we like it or not.

© 2004 SparkNotes LLC

A Pear of Tails

Homonyms are words that sound the same, even though they have different meanings, such as *pair* and *pear*.

Think of five sets of homonyms. For each set, think up a question and answer, possibly in the form of a joke, in which one homonym is confused with another.

To take the example of *pair* and *pear*, we might get: *Do you like eating pears? Sure, but I prefer eating triples.*

© 2004 SparkNotes LLC

The Danger of Mis-Punctuation

Donald J. Sobol's book *Encyclopedia Brown and the Case of the Missing Handprints* contains the story of Tyrone, a hopeless romantic, who writes the following love letter to his would-be girlfriend, Adorabelle:

How I long for a girl who understands what true romance is all about. You are sweet and faithful. Girls who are unlike you kiss the first boy who comes along, Adorabelle. I'd like to praise your beauty forever. I can't stop thinking you are the prettiest girl alive. Thine, Tyrone.

The trouble is, Tyrone dictates his letter over the phone to Adorabelle's young sister, who doesn't understand how punctuation works. She places punctuation marks in all the wrong places, so Adorabelle is furious when she reads the letter.

Repunctuate Tyrone's letter in such a way that it becomes insulting.

A Rule Up With Which I Will Not Put

Officially, it's incorrect to end sentences with **prepositions** (words like *of, for, with, at, to, in, from, up,* and so on). But many people think it's okay to break this rule. Sometimes sentences that *don't* end in prepositions sound extremely awkward. For example:

For what did you come here?

He is the hottest guy on whom I have ever laid eyes.

We have much for which to be thankful.

That depends on in what you believe.

Rewrite the sentences above so that they sound less stilted. Then think of three other sentences that will sound clunky unless they end in prepositions.

© 2004 SparkNotes LLC

How Many Words in the Alphabet?

In the next five minutes, see how many words you can come up with that contain some or all of the letters in the word *alphabet*.

Whr r th Vwls?

The ancient Hebrew alphabet contained no vowels. People reading Hebrew were expected to infer which vowel sounds occurred between consonants.

How would you handle an ancient Hebrew text? Try deciphering the following:

Wtht vwls, t cn b hrd t fllw wht smn hs wrttn. Vwls ccr cmmnly n wrttn nglsh. S y cn s, t cn b qt cnfsng wtht thm!

DAILY SPARK · SPELLING & GRAMMAR

© 2004 SparkNotes LLC

Row, Row, Row the Cow

Two words share a **visual rhyme** if they end in the same letters but sound different. For example, *row* (as in what you do with a boat) and *cow* (as in the animal) look like they should rhyme, but, in fact, they sound quite different from one another.

In the next five minutes, draw up a list of as many visual rhymes as possible.

© 2004 SparkNotes LLC

We Run Over to the Playground in Order to Run Wild

Many verbs can be used for a variety of purposes. For example, the verb *run* can be used to say all sorts of different things. We can run across the street, run wild, run away, or run for political office, or our nose can run, and so on.

For each of the following verbs, come up with five different uses that differ significantly. For example, *run across the street* differs significantly from *run for political office*, but it is pretty similar to *run around the track*.

catch
beat
look
find
do

© 2004 SparkNotes LLC

Pit Bulls and Pears

Suppose to is a made-up phrase. When we're talking, we often say *suppose to* instead of the grammatically correct *supposed to*, which is why people sometimes use the phrase *suppose to* in their writing.

To burn the correct phrase into your brain, write four sentences that use *supposed to*. Write one sentence about pit bulls, one sentence about politicians, one sentence about protractors, and one sentence about pears.

© 2004 SparkNotes LLC

4² Words

The following square of sixteen letters contains eight words: four spelled left to right and four spelled top to bottom.

```
B  E  T  A
L  A  R  D
U  S  E  D
E  Y  E  S
```

In the next five minutes, try to form a square of sixteen letters containing as many words as you can. Five is good, six is very good, seven is excellent, and eight is perfect.

© 2004 SparkNotes LLC

DAILY SPARK

SPELLING & GRAMMAR

© 2004 SparkNotes LLC

How Many Ways Can You Mark Up a Sentence?

Make a list of all the punctuation marks you can think of. Then write a short paragraph in which you use each punctuation mark once and only once. If you have trouble, give yourself permission to use the comma and the period more than once.

Too Loopy for Words

The following words form a loop (the list begins and ends with *car*), where each word is in some way related to the words next to it, but is unrelated to the words next to its neighbors: *car, horn, goat, grass, lawnmower, engine, car.*

In the next five minutes, brainstorm three different word loops, each containing between five and eight words.

© 2004 SparkNotes LLC

Me Talk Like a Caveman

Let's get this straight: *I* designates the subject of the sentence; *me* designates the object. An easy way to figure out if *I* or *me* is correct is to remove the other person from the sentence, and then check to see if the sentence still makes sense. For example, *Me and Jaime went out last night.* That sounds fine in speech, but take away *Jaime*, and you're left with *Me went out last night.* That sounds wrong, so you know that *I*, not *me*, is correct.

Write a paragraph detailing the last great Saturday night you and your best friend had. Begin every single sentence with _____ **and I**.

© 2004 SparkNotes LLC

Some of the Same

The consonants *t* and *b* can be turned into a variety of different words by inserting different vowels in different places. For instance, you could come up with *tub*, *tube*, *tuba*, or *tab*.

See how many words you can come up with by inserting vowels into each of the following strings of consonants: *gr, str, lt, sw, cd*.

© 2004 SparkNotes LLC

Backwords

Shouldn't it make sense that spelling something backward should mean its opposite? For instance, shouldn't *doog* mean "bad," since *doog* is *good* backward?

Invent five new words by spelling common words backward to mean their opposite.

© 2004 SparkNotes LLC

Crack the Anagram

An **anagram** is a word that has been formed by rearranging the letters of another word. For example, *silent* is an anagram for *listen*.

Each word in the following sentence has been rearranged into an anagram. See if you can piece together the original sentence.

Ethos eel pope ta snake sport ruse era gater.

Hint: *eel pope* and *snake sport* are each anagrams for a single word.

© 2004 SparkNotes LLC

DAILY SPARK

SPELLING & GRAMMAR

© 2004 SparkNotes LLC

The 200-Pound Moustache

Misplaced modifiers are single words, phrases, or clauses that do not point clearly to the word or words they modify.

Rewrite the following sentences, all of which contain misplaced modifiers, so that they make sense:

The actor was a tall man with a red moustache weighing 200 pounds.

The teacher posted the times for the students discussed in class.

Definitely the most convenient method of travel, Jimmy took the subway to work.

I was told that Maurice sent me flowers by my mother.

Sailing toward the floor, Grandma Tina caught the martini glass.

Many More Problems

Many is a **plain adjective**: *I have many ideas. More* is a **comparative adjective**: *I have many more ideas than you do.*

Fill in the blanks with *more* or *many*:

I have _____ time to sleep on the weekends.

I don't have _____ hours left before class.

Zelda has _____ problems. However, Scott has even _____ problems than she does.

Hal owns _____ records than Harry, but Harry has _____ MP3s.

© 2004 SparkNotes LLC

A Tough Thought

The four-letter combination *ough* occurs in a variety of different words. Brainstorm as many words as you can think of that contain *ough*.

How many different pronunciations can you find for *ough*?

© 2004 SparkNotes LLC

Neither Easy nor Hard

Neither . . . nor and *either . . . or* seem to be referring to two different things, but watch out—*neither* and *either* are singular pronouns, and they require singular verbs.

Test your comprehension of *neither . . . nor* and *either . . . or* by using them to combine the following sentences:

Jonas isn't coming tonight. Marianne also isn't coming.

Tonight's program could be Bach. It could also be Beethoven.

Houses can be built from wood. They can also be built from brick.

Fox News is inaccurate. CNN is also pretty biased.

Gordon doesn't like Chinese food. Sally also doesn't like Chinese food.

© 2004 SparkNotes LLC

Batman and I

Fill in the blanks in each of the following sentences twice. The first time, fill in the blanks as if you did everything. The second time, fill in the blanks as if you and Batman did everything.

_____ have the fastest car in the world.

There's nothing quite like a mug of hot chocolate to make _____ feel content.

I wish the Joker would quit making fun of _____ pet dog.

You want everyone to believe that this utility belt is yours, but you know perfectly well that it's _____.

Do you notice any similarity between the first time through and the second?

© 2004 SparkNotes LLC

Mangled Reports

Below is a list of real sentences included in traffic reports, as compiled in a book called *Anguished English* by Richard Lederer. For each sentence, write two sentences, one that expresses what you think the person writing the report intended, and one that expresses a possible alternative reading of the sentence.

"In an attempt to kill a fly, I drove into a telephone pole."

"The guy was all over the road. I had to swerve several times before I hit him."

"The other car collided with mine without giving any warning of its intention."

"A pedestrian hit me and went under my car."

"I had been driving for forty years when I fell asleep at the wheel and had an accident."

© 2004 SparkNotes LLC

© 2004 SparkNotes LLC

Uninterested in the Difference

Contrary to popular belief, *uninterested* and *disinterested* do not mean the same thing. *Uninterested* means "not interested"; *disinterested* means "impartial" or "objective."

Fill in the blanks with *uninterested* or *disinterested*:

Hector, an excellent judge, is always _____.
Helen is completely _____ in dating Hector.
George and Martha called on a trusted, _____ friend to settle their dispute.
Far from being _____, Corzine welcomes bribes and _____ is in fairness.
_____ in the circus, Garrett read a book as the clowns performed.

Can You BeLIEve It?

Many words, especially longer ones, contain other words within them. For example, the name *SparkNotes* contains numerous words: *spa, spar, spark, stars, to, toes, tone, torn, on, pant, par, park, pass, rant, rest, a, ark, knot, no, not, note,* and *notes.*

In the next five minutes, brainstorm as many words as you can think of that contain at least three other words. What's the greatest number of words you can find contained in another word?

© 2004 SparkNotes LLC

Run Up to a Run Around

Often, a verb and preposition combine to form an expression that differs from the standard meaning of the verb. For example, we can say that something *falls under* a particular category, even though the verb *fall* normally has to do with things giving in to the influence of gravity.

See how many expressions you can form by combining the following verbs and prepositions. For each expression, provide a sentence that demonstrates its meaning.

go	*around*
run	*off*
call	*down*
give	*up*
shoot	*out*

© 2004 SparkNotes LLC

Get On Top of the Top

Many words can be used as different parts of speech carrying different meanings. For example, the noun *produce* means farm products, especially fruits and vegetables, while the verb *produce* means something similar to "create."

Think up five words that can be used as more than one part of speech. For each pair of words, compose a sentence that contains both words.

© 2004 SparkNotes LLC

Mary Mary, Quite Contrary

A **contronym** is a word that can be used to have two opposite meanings. For instance, *out* is a contronym: when we write *The moon is out*, we mean the moon is visible, but when we write *The lights are out*, we mean that they are not visible.

For each of the following words, compose two sentences in which the word is used with two opposite meanings: *buckle, left, oversight, screen*.

© 2004 SparkNotes LLC

Looking for Opposites

The prefixes *in-* and *dis-*, when added to words, often give them an opposite meaning. For example, the opposite of *tolerant* is *intolerant*, and the opposite of *loyal* is *disloyal*.

We all know what *disgusting* means, but what about *gusting*? For each of the following words, remove the *in-* or *dis-* to create a new word, which presumably has an opposite meaning. Then define each new word.

disgruntled	distress
insert	infect
disparage	discreet
distort	indignant
insolent	inquire

DAILY SPARK SPELLING & GRAMMAR

© 2004 SparkNotes LLC

There They're Happy About Their Good Grammar

The words *their, they're,* and *there* are by no means interchangeable—although some people use them as if they are. *Their* is possessive (*They lost their hearts in San Francisco*); *they're* is the contraction of *they are* (*They're going to get married*); and *there* refers to location (*There is the church*).

Write six sentences, two of which use *their,* two of which use *they're,* and two of which use *there.*

© 2004 SparkNotes LLC

Reading, Writing, and Arithmeticing

Errors in **parallelism** occur when sentences do not start, continue, and end in the same way. It's especially common to find errors of parallelism in sentences that list actions or items. For example, *Uta enjoys fancy restaurants, diners, and eating at cafés.* Instead of continuing to list nouns like *restaurants* and *diners*, the writer throws an *-ing* word into the mix (*eating*). To match the other nouns, the last part of the sentence should read *and cafés.*

Try writing four sentences that include lists; make sure to avoid parallelism errors.

© 2004 SparkNotes LLC

Just Between the Two of Us

Use *between* to describe exactly two things: *On the flight to Tampa, passengers chose between salmon and chicken.* Use *among* to describe two or more countable things: *At the wedding, guests chose among salmon, chicken, and vegetarian lasagna.* Use *amid* to describe things that cannot be counted: *They wandered amid the wreckage of dinner.* Avoid *amongst* and *amidst* in all circumstances, unless you are trying out for an episode of *Masterpiece Theatre*.

Fill in the blanks with *between, among,* or *amid:*

Elinor had to choose _____ four suitors.
Louis walked _____ the black and the red buildings.
I felt at peace sitting _____ my five closest friends in the world.
Greg strolled _____ the trees all night.
Jessie can never choose _____ the peach and the mango sorbets.

Tea Time (In Parentheses)

Use **parentheses** to include nonessential material in a sentence. For example, *The children arrived home at six o'clock (tea time)*. Too many parenthetical interruptions will disrupt the flow of your writing, so try to avoid using them.

Capitalizing and punctuating within parentheses is simple. Any punctuation belonging to the main sentence goes outside the parentheses. Even if the stuff inside the parentheses is a complete sentence, the punctuation always goes outside the parentheses if it's part of another sentence: *With a shudder, Eileen turned away from Gavi (she couldn't bear to look at him)*.

Write four sentences using parentheses. Then rewrite two of them without the parentheses, incorporating the parenthetical material into the main body of the sentence.

© 2004 SparkNotes LLC

Screaming and Fretting

Participles and **gerunds** both often end in *-ing*, so they're easy to confuse. But a participle is a **verbal** (a word that has the characteristics of both a verb and a noun or adjective) used as an adjective, as in *the screaming child* or *the fretting mother*. In this sentence, *shouting* is a participle, because it modifies *the man*: *Shouting, the man raced across the room.*

Write four sentences that include participles.

© 2004 SparkNotes LLC

A Beginning and an Ending

See how many different words you can form with these strings of letters by adding one letter to the beginning and one letter to the ending of them:

rap

are

lam

ose

© 2004 SparkNotes LLC

© 2004 SparkNotes LLC

Pox, Politics, and Beans

Subject-verb agreement can be tricky when you're dealing with words that look plural but are actually singular. These words mostly fall in the category of diseases (*mumps, measles, rickets, chicken pox*), academic disciplines (*mathematics, physics, ethics, politics, economics*), and certain foods (*baked beans*).

Write three sentences expressing your opinions about chicken pox, politics, and baked beans. Make sure you match these nouns with singular verbs.

My Money Is Mine

Possessive pronouns show who owns something. The following pronouns are possessives: *my, mine, your, yours, his, her, hers, its, our, ours, their,* and *theirs.*

Write a paragraph about your most prized possession. Use as many possessive pronouns as possible.

© 2004 SparkNotes LLC

Moving Prepositions Around

Find a way of rephrasing each of the following sentences so that they no longer end with a preposition:

That looks like a nice trail, but it's not in the direction of the lake we're heading toward.

That's quite a mess you seem to have found yourself in.

Which town are you coming from?

She's the best person to play basketball with.

You have no idea what you're talking about.

© 2004 SparkNotes LLC

He or He?

When using **pronouns** (words like *he, she, they,* and so on), be sure your reader knows what those pronouns are referring to. Confusion can easily arise, especially if you're talking about two men or two women.

Rewrite the following sentences so that the pronouns refer to one antecedent:

Melissa's mom told her she thought she was too fat.

Mike and Peter played baseball; he hit a home run.

When Janie and Melanie went to lunch, she confessed that she had kissed Hank the night before.

George told Simon that he wanted to leave the party early.

© 2004 SparkNotes LLC

One Should Not Shift Your Pronouns

A **pronoun shift** occurs when a writer starts out using one pronoun, then suddenly shifts and starts using another. For example, *If they want to succeed in business, you have to play by the rules.* In this sentence, the writer first uses the **third-person pronoun** *they* but then changes to the **second-person pronoun** *you.*

Rewrite the following sentences, getting rid of the pronoun shifts:

If you plan to attend the picnic, they each need to bring a few sandwiches.

When we were learning French, the most important thing you did was study grammar every day.

If one is attending a dinner party, you should remember not to eat too much in the afternoon.

123   DAILY SPARK   SPELLING & GRAMMAR   © 2004 SparkNotes LLC

His, Her, or Their

Pronouns must always match the words they replace. For some writers, this rule poses problems when **indefinite pronouns** enter the picture. Just remember that indefinite pronouns (words like *anyone, everyone, someone, no one, nobody* and so on) are always singular. For example, *Everyone must bring his or her lunch to school.*

Write a paragraph describing the ideal student dress code. Use all of the indefinite pronouns listed above.

© 2004 SparkNotes LLC

Us Girls

To practice correct pronoun usage, rewrite the following sentences correctly. Be careful: not all will need rewriting.

Gail gave a really nice dictionary to George and me.

Us girls love to go out dancing.

Claire and him got in a huge fight last night.

Are Eduardo and her coming to dinner later?

© 2004 SparkNotes LLC

Student Bloopers

School is a stressful place, and our brains aren't always 100 percent on the task. Occasionally, students make errors with surprising double meanings.

Each of the following, listed courtesy of *Anguished English*, by Richard Lederer, is something a student actually wrote. Rewrite each sentence in a way that makes the intended meaning clear.

"It is bad manners to break your bread and roll in your soup."

"In Tennessee Williams's *The Glass Menagerie*, Laura's leg keeps coming between her and other people."

"The president of the United States, in having foreign affairs, has to have the consent of the Senate."

"When Lincoln was president, he wore only a tall silk hat."

"During the Napoleonic Wars, the crowned heads of Europe were trembling in their shoes."

© 2004 SparkNotes LLC

© 2004 SparkNotes LLC

Modify This

Each of the following is a real sentence that has appeared in print. For each sentence, draw a cartoon that illustrates the misunderstanding created by the **misplaced modifier**.

Two cars were reported stolen by the police yesterday.
Please take time to look over the brochure that is enclosed with your family.
Locked in a vault for fifty years, the owner of the jewels decided to sell them.
The patient was referred to a psychiatrist with a severe emotional problem.
The athlete soaked an ankle he injured in an ice bucket.

Where Do You Put the Spaces?

The string of letters below can be turned into a sentence by inserting spaces and punctuation marks. As it turns out, there are two possible sentences that you can create, depending on where you put the spaces and punctuation marks. Neither sentence makes much sense, but both are grammatically correct. Can you create both sentences?

WHEREVERYOUTANDOUTTERRESTTRIALSGOADAMATEURCHINS

© 2004 SparkNotes LLC

No Bear Feet Allowed

Two words with similar spelling or pronunciation often have very different meanings.

For each of the following pairs of words, compose a sentence in which one word is mistakenly used instead of the other. For example, by confusing *bear* and *bare*, you might create a sentence that reads *No bear feet allowed*. The double meaning implies that no one with the feet of a bear is allowed.

Use a dictionary if you aren't sure what the following words mean: *complement/compliment*, *ballet/ballot*, *wrench/wench*, *conversation/conservation*, *steel/steal*.

© 2004 SparkNotes LLC

Less Is Fewer

With which of the following would you use the word *fewer*? With which of the following would you use the word *less*?

alcohol
bread
car
oxygen
particle
seed
spaceship
spoon
sugar
water

DAILY SPARK SPELLING & GRAMMAR

© 2004 SparkNotes LLC

© 2004 SparkNotes LLC

God Threw the Tip of the Dog in the Pit

In the next five minutes, brainstorm as many pairs of words as you can in which one word spelled backward makes the other word. What's the longest pair of words you can come up with?

Some Words Are Longer Than Others

Try composing a sentence of at least ten words in which none of the words is longer than four letters. Now try composing a sentence of at least ten words in which none of the words is shorter than five letters. Which sentence was more difficult to write?

© 2004 SparkNotes LLC

A Difficult Sentence to Write

Write two sentences describing a recent visit you paid to the planet Jupiter. In the first sentence, make every word come later in alphabetical order than the one before it. In the second sentence, make every word come earlier in alphabetical order than the one before it.

© 2004 SparkNotes LLC

DAILY SPARK SPELLING & GRAMMAR

Rules to Live By

The columnist William Safire has made a list of self-violating spelling and grammar rules. Rewrite each rule so that it doesn't violate itself.

"Remember to never split an infinitive."

"The passive voice should never be used."

"Place pronouns as close as possible, especially in long sentences, as of ten or more words, to their antecedents."

"If any word is improper at the end of a sentence, a linking verb is."

"Everyone should be careful to use a singular pronoun with singular nouns in their writing."

© 2004 SparkNotes LLC

An International Language

There are roughly 115 countries in the world in which English has some sort of official recognition. Many of these countries have large numbers of native speakers of English who, over time, have developed their own distinctive dialects of English, with their own turns of phrase, vocabulary, and grammar.

Try to guess the meaning of the italicized words from other dialects of English:

The man behind the desk was wearing *opticals*. (India)
She was dressed beautifully, and her *eartops* brought out her eyes. (Pakistan)
Don't check your homework with him; he's so *blur*. (Singapore)
I have to work on Saturday, or I'll get in trouble with my *baas*. (South Africa)
I got this black eye in a *barney*. (Australia)
Isn't it *gas* how many different dialects of English there are? (Ireland)
It's pretty cold out; you might want to put on your *tuque*. (Canada)
He doesn't mince his words; he's very *hard*. (Anguilla)

© 2004 SparkNotes LLC

Build a Word One Letter at a Time

Divide into partners or small groups to play the following spelling game.

Randomly select someone to go first. That person says a letter of the alphabet. Then take turns going back and forth (or in a circle with a group of more than two), saying one letter each. The object is to spell a word, but not to be the person who gives the last letter of the word.

If you aren't sure how to go on, you can always bluff by adding a letter without having any idea of a word that could be formed by it. If you think the person before you is bluffing, you can challenge that person. If that person has a word in mind, then you lose the point. If that person was bluffing, then he or she loses the point.

© 2004 SparkNotes LLC

© 2004 SparkNotes LLC

Basically Everyone Should Really . . .

In your writing, strive for accuracy, but don't qualify every other assertion with words like *rather, mostly, little, extremely, kind of, really,* and so on. Overuse of **qualifiers** like these will weaken your writing. Rewrite the following paragraph, removing all qualifiers:

Although almost everyone should be allowed to sleep pretty much whenever he or she wants, I basically draw the line at going to bed at three in the afternoon. My boyfriend, Gabe, completely refuses to go to sleep at an even slightly normal time: he fully insists on staying awake until he completely passes out from exhaustion. His mother doesn't really care, but I usually can't at all stand going out with a guy with such a totally irregular schedule.

Are You Asking a Question?

Be careful not to misuse **question marks**. Sentences that simply *describe* questions, without actually *asking* questions, should end with periods. For example, the sentence *Bruce wondered how much more he could take* should end with a period, because it describes Bruce's wondering. The sentence *How much more can I take?* should end with a question mark, because it directly asks a question.

Repunctuate the following sentences if they are incorrectly punctuated:

After all, what is this film but a collection of car chases.

Victor asked me what I was doing later?

I wondered how you're coping with your mother's illness.

Why did Preston come here, if all he planned to do was whine and complain.

© 2004 SparkNotes LLC

Go! Order! Rinse! Erase!

Divide into partners or small groups. Randomly select someone to go first. That person will say a verb. The next person must then say a verb that starts with the same letter that the previous verb ended with, and so on. See how many verbs you can think of before one of you gets stuck.

© 2004 SparkNotes LLC

"A Chapter" in *A Book*

Use **quotation marks** around the titles of songs, short poems, essays, one-act plays, and other short literary works. Quotation marks are also used to mark parts of a whole, such as chapter in books; articles in newspapers, magazines, journals, or other periodicals; and episodes of television or radio series. *Italicize* or <u>underline</u> major works: books, television series, full-length albums, magazines, and feature-length films.

In the following sentences, italicize or put quotation marks around the works of art:

My dad took me to see Gladiator at Union Square.

Andrew's favorite episode of the TV show Fawlty Towers is called The Kipper and the Corpse.

Lila always listens to the Beatles' song I'm Still Sleeping, which is on the album Revolver.

I read a really interesting article in the New York Times Magazine called Fixing Nemo.

© 2004 SparkNotes LLC

Happy Together

Some nouns attach to verbs in a way that alters their meaning slightly. For example, you don't have a good laugh or have a fit in quite the same way that you have money or cars or friends.

Alter the meaning of each of the following verbs in as many ways as you can by attaching different nouns to them. One noun is given in parentheses next to each verb to give you a sense of what's intended.

get (a lucky break)
give (a deep groan)
make (a comment)
take (aim)
catch (a cold)

© 2004 SparkNotes LLC

An Everyday Occurrence

Believe it or not, *everyday* and *every day* mean two different things. Advertisements use the two phrases interchangeably (*Go the Distance Everyday*), but they shouldn't. *Everyday* means "ordinary" or "usual"; *every day* is used to indicate something that happens each day.

Write four sentences, two of which use *everyday* and two of which use *every day*.

© 2004 SparkNotes LLC

I Love Semicolons; Consequently, I Use Them A Lot

Use **semicolons** to link two independent clauses. Sometimes the semicolon alone will get the job done (*I am leaving Larissa's house; I will never return*); sometimes, you'll want to use a **conjunctive adverb** like *however, moreover, therefore, consequently, otherwise, nevertheless,* or *thus* along with the semicolon (*I hate Larissa; therefore, I am leaving her house forever*).

Write four sentences about your weekend, two of which use semicolons alone and two of which use semicolons with conjunctive adverbs.

© 2004 SparkNotes LLC

Got a Bee in Your Bonnet?

The word *beekeeper* contains five *e*'s. In the next five minutes, brainstorm as many words as you can that repeat one letter three or more times.

© 2004 SparkNotes LLC

Pros and Cons

When we weigh a decision, we often talk about pros and cons. The **pros** are factors in favor of a decision and the **cons** are factors against it. So the words *pro* and *con* are opposites. *Pro-* and *con-* are also common prefixes, which often give words opposite meanings. For example, *to contract* means "to shrink" and *to protract* means "to stretch out" or "to extend."

Think of five words that begin either with *pro-* or *con-*. Invent a new word by replacing the *con-* with a *pro-* or the *pro-* with a *con-*.

Once you have completed this exercise, see if you can deduce what the opposite of *progress* must be.

© 2004 SparkNotes LLC

Wouldn't You Know It

In **contractions**, the **apostrophe** (') indicates that a letter (or letters) has been omitted. The most common contractions are those that combine a pronoun and a verb (*she's, you're, they're,* and so on) or a verb and the word *not* (*don't, wouldn't, won't,* and so on).

Rewrite the following sentences, using contractions where possible:

Jake is the loveliest guy I have ever met.
I will not go to the party unless you come with me.
We are happy to see you.
I cannot believe how fat that cat has gotten.
Jean had not prepared for Alice's departure.
You should not stay out all night before an exam.
Andrew did not stay long at the restaurant.
I have not had time to study.

© 2004 SparkNotes LLC

Love It, Hate It, or Tolerate It

People have strong feelings about the **serial comma**, that little mark that precedes the final conjunction in a list. Fans of the serial comma write sentences like this: *Richard lay awake worrying about the mortgage, the kids, and his ulcer.* Non-fans would write the same sentence this way: *Richard lay awake worrying about the mortgage, the kids and his ulcer.*

Are you for or against the serial comma? Decide, then write five sentences that demonstrate your preference.

© 2004 SparkNotes LLC

The Sounds of Silence

The letter *e* often is often unpronounced when it appears at the ends of words. We don't pronounce the *e* at the end of *pronounce*, for instance. Other letters are also occasionally silent. We don't normally think of the letter *n* as silent, but it is in the word *autumn*.

In the next five minutes, go through the alphabet and, for each letter, see how many words you can think of in which that letter is not pronounced.

© 2004 SparkNotes LLC

Don't Be Left Defenseless

In the next five minutes, make a list of words that contain only one vowel, but repeat that vowel at least twice. What's the longest such word you can think of?

Right Versus Left

In standard typing practice, the left hand will cover the letters *q, w, e, r, t, a, s, d, f, g, z, x, c, v,* and *b*, while the right hand will cover the letters *y, u, i, o, p, h, j, k, l, n,* and *m*.

Think of some words you could type using only your left hand and then some words you could type using only your right hand. Note that it's much more difficult to spell words with only the right hand.

© 2004 SparkNotes LLC

Crack the Code

The paragraph below has been written in a code in which every letter has been replaced by another letter. See if you can crack the code. Some hints to get started: *E* is the most common letter in the alphabet. Every word contains at least one vowel. *The* is the most commonly occurring word in English. There are only two words that have only one letter, *a* and *I*. *A* is usually not capitalized, and *I* is always capitalized. Give it a go!

Fqc ycmf blg fi wdlws l winc jm fi mfldf bjfq l ocb olejtjld ctceczlm. Flsc l ocb phcmmcm lyihf fqc tcffcdm fqlf wiec hk ahjfc iofcz, lzn odie fqimc phcmmcm, mcc jo gih wlz kjcwc fipcfqcd l ocb io fqc bidnm. Mtibtg yhf mhdctg, gih'tt bids ihf fqc eclzjzpm io eidc lzn sidc tcffcdm. Jf elg yc mtib pijzp lf ojdmf, yhf lm gih elsc jzdilnm jf bjtt ycwiec clmjcd lzn clmjcd.

To Boldly Split Infinitives

Split infinitives occur when a word is placed between *to* and a verb. For example, *to aggressively move, to delicately leap, to slowly understand*. Technically, splitting infinitives is against the rules, but many people think this rule is a little outdated.

Sometimes, for the sake of emphasis or clarity, you might want to break up an infinitive. Just be sure you're making a style choice, rather than a mistake.

Write four sentences, two with intact infinitives and two with split infinitves.

© 2004 SparkNotes LLC

© 2004 SparkNotes LLC

Eh Bigge Misstake

Rewrite this paragraph, misspelling every word. The trick, however, is that you have to misspell the words in such a way that someone reading the paragraph would still be able to make out what it means.

An Excellent Experience

Brainstorm words that contain the letter *x*. Are there any patterns to the kinds of words you come up with?

DAILY SPARK SPELLING & GRAMMAR

© 2004 SparkNotes LLC

Catch the Misspellings

In the paragraph below, ten words are italicized. Five of them are spelled correctly and five of them are spelled incorrectly. See if you can figure out which of the five are spelled incorrectly and correct their spelling.

Adolesence is a time of growing *independence* in a person's life. There can *definately* be plenty of *embarrassment,* but it can also be a time of joy, even *ecstasy.* The new *millennium* will be not just a *repitition* of the old: it will offer all sorts of new opportunities for teenagers to find their own voices and make sense of their own *existances.* These new opportunities may seem to make only a *miniscule* difference, but they may well create more room for self-expression, safe from the harsh *judgment* of others.

© 2004 SparkNotes LLC

The Effect on the Subject

Always make sure that the subject and verb of every sentence that you write match (this is called **subject-verb agreement**). If the subject is singular, then the verb must be singular too. If the subject is plural, ditto for the verb.

Choose the correct verb in the following sentences:

The speaker the students heard yesterday <u>was/were</u> one of the congressmen from Wisconsin.

Neither the judge nor the jury <u>is/are</u> at fault.

Even though the effects of eating french fries <u>is/are</u> well known, many people can't resist the greasy treat.

Next to the perfume aisle, on top of a forgotten shelf, <u>sit/sits</u> a dusty mitten.

© 2004 SparkNotes LLC

Sing Along, Write a Longer

Write down the lyrics (or as much as you can remember) of a pop song of your choice. Now rewrite the lyrics in the form of a business letter—that is, use paragraph form and formal English, complete with correct spelling and punctuation, no slang, and no rhymes or verse forms.

© 2004 SparkNotes LLC

Don't Pause for Breath!

Without violating any rules of grammar, and without redundancy (you can't simply write *very* fifty times over), try to write the longest sentence you can. How many words can you manage?

© 2004 SparkNotes LLC

Defragmentation

Turn the following **fragments** (incomplete sentences) into grammatically correct sentences:

The loud stereo that kept me up all night.

The gorgeous sunrise breaking on the horizon.

The obnoxious child only a mother could love.

Reading *The Great Gatsby* until dawn.

While the mother stood outside waiting.

DAILY SPARK SPELLING & GRAMMAR

© 2004 SparkNotes LLC

I Was Changing My Tense, When . . .

To avoid bewildering your readers, be sure to keep the **tense** of your verbs consistent.

Rewrite the following paragraph to eliminate confusing tense shifts:

We decided to go to Italy and had chosen Capri as our destination. John, who loved swimming, had always wanted to swim in the ocean around Capri. There had been a huge rainstorm the night before we reached our hotel, so when we arrive the streets are still wet. John wants to visit the Blue Grotto right away, but I wanted to unpack. I changed into my swimsuit when a goat walks right into our room!

DAILY SPARK

SPELLING & GRAMMAR

© 2004 SparkNotes LLC

A Definite Study

In the next five minutes, brainstorm as many words as you can that contain three consecutive letters of the alphabet in a row. For example, *definite* contains the letters *d*, *e*, and *f* all in a row, while *study* contains *s*, *t*, and *u* all in a row.

Can you think of any words that contain four consecutive letters of the alphabet?

© 2004 SparkNotes LLC

Give Me a Call

The numbers on a telephone's keypad have letters associated with them as follows: 2 is *a-b-c*, 3 is *d-e-f*, 4 is *g-h-i*, 5 is *j-k-l*, 6 is *m-n-o*, 7 is *p-r-s*, 8 is *t-u-v*, 9 is *w-x-y*, and 0 is sometimes *q* and *z*. Businesses often use these letters to make their numbers easier to remember. For example, it's much easier to remember the number 1-800-COLLECT than it is to remember 1-800-265-5328.

See if you can find any catchy words spelled in your phone number. Then see if you can do the same for the phone numbers of friends or other numbers you're familiar with.

© 2004 SparkNotes LLC

If You're Confused, Then You're Sillier Than I Thought

Than and *then* are easily confused. Although the words sound similar, their meanings are entirely different. Use *than* for making comparisons: *Andrea is prettier than her sister.* Use *then* when time is involved: *First you moisturize, and then you apply foundation.*

Fill in the blanks with *then* or *than*:

If you think Sharon's smart, _____ you're insane.

Geraldine arrived, _____ Allan showed up.

I ate breakfast; _____ I went for a run.

I would rather eat breakfast _____ go running.

My Friend, the Letter *B*

Pick a letter of the alphabet, and then write a paragraph introducing this letter to others. Describe the qualities you associate with the letter, and explain why it is you like this letter. You may also give this letter some gentle criticism if you think it has particular shortcomings.

© 2004 SparkNotes LLC

Avoiding the Top Ten

According to the annual *Guinness Book of World Records*, the ten most frequently used words in the English language are, in order, *the, of, and, to, a, in, that, is, I,* and *it*.

Write a paragraph explaining how it came to pass that yesterday you grew more than thirty feet and went on a rampage through your hometown. See if you can do it without using any of the ten words mentioned above. If you can't manage that, aim to use as few of these top ten words as possible.

© 2004 SparkNotes LLC

A Family of Homonyms

The three words *their, they're,* and *there* are all pronounced the same, and they are often confused. Write a sentence using all three of the words correctly.

DAILY SPARK SPELLING & GRAMMAR

© 2004 SparkNotes LLC

Word Scramble

Each of the following are a string of words that has been scrambled. For each string of words, try to unscramble the words in three different ways to create three different grammatically correct sentences. Insert any punctuation marks you like.

blue the room light the over brightly shines

whistle gave his the grandson old to man the

meet I'm york going friend in new to best my

wind late the clock it before gets

say what when you did here you get

© 2004 SparkNotes LLC

Eventually, We Used Transitions

Transitions are the sentences or words that aid readers in following the flow of your writing. Transitions can be used to:

Show contrast: Jesse starts his homework after school. <u>In contrast</u>, Evan watches TV.

Elaborate: I ordered nachos. <u>In addition</u>, I asked for a large soda.

Provide an example: There are many treasures at that thrift store. <u>For example</u>, Patricia recently bought a cool lamp shade and a vintage wedding dress.

Show results: Britney ate nothing but ice cream and buffalo wings every day for a month. <u>As a result</u>, she gained ten pounds.

Show sequence: The police busted up Arun's party. <u>Soon after</u>, his parents grounded him, and <u>eventually</u> Arun ran away from home.

Come up with four new sentence pairs, using a different kind of transition in each.

© 2004 SparkNotes LLC

Everybody Fills in His or Her Blanks

Remember, some words seem to be plural, even though they're actually singular. *Everyone, everybody,* and *each* fall into this category.

Fill in the blanks with a correct verb form and, if necessary, a pronoun:

Each of the cars in that lot _____ a red stripe across the hood.

Everybody in the concert hall _____ wearing a suit.

Each and every student _____ responsible for _____ own actions.

Everyone in the café _____ unhappy with _____ dinner.

© 2004 SparkNotes LLC

A Pluralist Society

Most nouns are made plural according to a simple rule: add *s* to the singular form. However, there are plenty of exceptions to this rule; we don't say *geeses* or *mouses*, for example.

Think of as many different rules for making a noun plural as you can, providing at least one example for each rule.

DAILY SPARK SPELLING & GRAMMAR

© 2004 SparkNotes LLC

© 2004 SparkNotes LLC

Is There Enough *Is* in Your Life?

The word *is* has many different uses. The *is* of identity is like an equals sign: it says that what's on one side of the *is* is the same as what's on the other side. For example, in the sentence *Paris is the capital of France*, *Paris* and *the capital of France* are two names for the same thing. The *is* of predication is used to qualify or modify what goes before the *is*. For example, in the sentence *Paris is full of historical sites*, we learn what is being said about Paris by reading what comes after the *is*. The *is* of existence is used, as the name suggests, to say that something exists. *There is a city called Paris* is an example of this kind of *is*.

Rewrite each of the following sentences replacing each *is* with *i-is* if it's an *is* of identity, with *p-is* if it's an *is* of predication, and with *e-is* if it's an *is* of existence.

Is there enough time to drop by my house on the way?
She is the youngest person ever to win a gold medal in archery.
Andy, the new team captain, is really responsible.

Three, Two, One, Sentence!

Arrange the following words so that they form three coherent sentences:

and care concerned do hurt I I might not seem that think you you

Now rearrange the same words so that they form two coherent sentences. Then rearrange the same words so that they form one coherent sentence.

DAILY SPARK SPELLING & GRAMMAR

© 2004 SparkNotes LLC

© 2004 SparkNotes LLC

Who? What? When? Where? Why? How?

The six words *who, what, when, where, why,* and *how* are often called "question words," because they are commonly used to ask questions. But not every sentence that uses these words is a question. We can write *Tell me what you did today* or *She knows why I wasn't there,* for example.

Compose five sentences, none of which are questions. In the first sentence, use two of the six question words. In the second, use three of the six question words, and so on, until in the fifth sentence you try to use all six question words.

Building a Pyramid

The letters to the right form a word pyramid:

```
                        T
              O                   A
        G           N           L
     A          S           K           L
```

You can follow any route from top to bottom, making diagonal jumps, and form a word. This pyramid contains the words, from left to right, *toga*, *togs*, *tons*, *tans*, *tank*, *talk*, and *tall*.

Four letters have been left blank in the word pyramid below. See if you can fill them in.

© 2004 SparkNotes LLC

DAILY SPARK

SPELLING & GRAMMAR

© 2004 SparkNotes LLC

Creating a Word Ladder

On the top of a sheet of paper, write a word of your choice, preferably one that's relatively simple. Then pass your sheet of paper on to the person next to you. You, in turn, will receive a sheet of paper from the person on the other side of you. Look at the word on the new sheet of paper you receive, and write a new word by adding one letter, removing one letter, or changing one of the letters. Then pass that sheet of paper on. As the ladder of words on each sheet of paper grows, try to avoid using any word that you see higher up on the ladder.

A Lot of Nonsense

Alot is one of those made-up words that many people use. It is never correct to write *alot*; always use *a lot* instead.

To memorize this rule, write five sentences using *a lot*.

© 2004 SparkNotes LLC

Which You Probably Know

Some people think that the distinction between *which* and *that* is going out of style. Until it does, use *that* for essential information in a description (*Jenny chose the dress that had the fewest holes*) and *which* for nonessential additions to a description (*The dress, which was cheap, is hanging in Jenny's closet*). If you're not sure which word is correct, here's a shortcut: if you see a comma, *which* is usually correct.

Fill in the blanks with *that* or *which*:

The computer _____ Charlie bought is green.

The computer, _____ comes in green, blue, and silver, appeals to children.

I dislike editorials _____ express racist opinions.

The editorial expressing racist opinions, _____ appeared in the student newspaper, angered everyone.

© 2004 SparkNotes LLC

Who Knows the Rule?

Who and *whom* are certainly confusing—even some experienced writers aren't sure when to use which. Here's an easy way to figure it out: if you could replace the *w*-word with *he, she,* or *they,* use *who* or *whoever.* If you could replace the *w*-word with *him, her,* or *them,* use *whom* or *whomever.*

If you're still confused, simply rephrase the sentence so that you can choose between *he* and *him.* For example, if you have the sentence *He is someone whom/who I consider a hero,* rephrase the sentence: *I consider him a hero.* Because you used *him,* you know that *whom* is correct.

Fill in the blanks with *who* or *whom*:

The person _____ hit my car should have to pay to fix the damages.
The people _____ have been standing in line the longest should get in first.

Give the movie tickets to _____ you like.
Give the movie tickets to _____ seems to want it most.

178

© 2004 SparkNotes LLC

Enough of This Craziness!!!

In formal English, there is never an occasion that calls for more than a single exclamation mark or a single question mark. In casual correspondence, like email or instant messaging, people often use multiple exclamation marks or question marks. There is a subtle but clear difference between what's expressed by writing *Isn't this crazy?*, *Isn't this crazy???*, and *Isn't this crazy?!*

Come up with rules for when different kinds of enthusiastic punctuation are called for and what distinguishes one form of enthusiastic punctuation from another.

© 2004 SparkNotes LLC

Ain't Nobody Happy

Double negatives are a grammar don't in English. If you see two negative words (*not, no, isn't, nobody,* and so on) next to each other, beware—you might have a double negative on your hands.

Rewrite the following sentences as necessary (not all sentences require changes):

Can't nobody stop me from dreaming.

Joe can't hardly wait for gym class.

It's impossible not to scream when you watch this movie.

There isn't no way to get a perfect score.

If Mama ain't happy, ain't nobody happy.

© 2004 SparkNotes LLC

Answers

1. Answers will vary.

2. Answers will vary, but some possibilities include: chest = czoecith, mouse = mnaops, care = **chaerrh**, lawn = llachgn.

3. Answers may vary on the first five but should resemble something like the following: "quire," "saiko," "him," "nite," "mur." The second five are spelled as follows: "school," "scheme," "rough," "leopard," "schizophrenia."

4. It's very difficult to read sentences when there's absolutely no punctuation whatever. It must have been very difficult for people trying to read before the invention of punctuation, don't you think? By inserting spaces, punctuation marks, and lowercase letters, this paragraph will become much easier to read. What a relief that will be!

5. The teacher administered the exam.
   The saleswoman chose Georgia's outfit.
   Barbarians invaded the city.

6. Answers will vary.

7. John did not tell Emily that there was not enough sugar and salt, but not without making her not feel not bad.

8. Answers will vary.

9. Answers will vary.

10. *dog* → *dot* → *cot* → *cat; jump* → *pump* → *pomp* → *poop* → *pool; cool* → *wool* → *wood* → *word* → *worm* → *warm*

11. Answers will vary. *Billowy* is the longest common word in which the letters are all in alphabetical order, and *spoonfeed* is the longest common word in which the letters are all in reverse alphabetical order.

12. Answers will vary.

13. Answers will vary.

14. Answers will vary.

15. Answers will vary.

16. Answers will vary. *Bookkeeper* is one example of a word with three sets of two letters in a row.

17. Answers will vary. *Uncopyrightable* is the longest word in the English language in which no letter is repeated.

18. Answers will vary.

19. Answers will vary.

20. Answers will vary.

21. Answers will vary.

22. The smiley face—:)—functions in much the same way as traditional punctuation marks. This is only the most common of a wide assortment of emoticons that clarify meaning or add emotional

shading to online communication. Examples and definitions of online punctuation marks will vary.

23. Answers will vary. *Latchstring* has six consonants in a row, and *queueing* has five vowels in a row.

24. Answers will vary. For instance, *strength* contains more letters than *aviator*.

25. Answers will vary.

26. The factory owner's huge donation did not <u>affect</u> the senator's vote against the Clean Air Act.
Scientists are still determining the long-term <u>effect</u>s of smoking.
Scientists study how smoking <u>affect</u>s the lungs.
A cause-and-<u>effect</u> relationship exists between exercise and weight loss.
The story of his childhood <u>affect</u>ed me deeply.
What <u>effect</u> do you think George's arrival will have on Vera?

27. Answers will vary.

28. The boy's bike cost twenty bucks.
Jenny's dog ran away yesterday.
The woman's speech made me sleepy.
That horse's left leg hurts.
Gwendolyn's umbrella broke in the strong winds.

29. Answers will vary.

30. Answers will vary.

31. Answers will vary. *E* is more common than *a*, so it should be easier to do without *a* than *e*.

32. Answers will vary.

33. Answers will vary.

34. Answers will vary.

35. The students' voices filled the auditorium.
    The lawyers' fees exceeded two million dollars.
    The dogs' barking kept me up all night.
    The soldiers' parents worried about their children.

36. Athens's architecture
    James's motorcycle
    Bette Davis's movies

37. *It's* replaces the *he's* and *she's*, while *its* replaces *his* and *her*.

38. I feel <u>bad</u> that Harriet wasn't invited.
    Rudolph dances <u>badly</u>, but at least he tries hard.
    The soup tasted <u>bad</u> on the first day and even worse on the second.
    You look really <u>bad</u>. When was the last time you slept?
    Ms. Kramer spells <u>badly</u>, so it's lucky she has a secretary.
    Roger wanted to see Gisele so <u>badly</u> that he postponed his flight.

39. Answers will vary.

40. <u>Your</u> son has a serious behavior problem, probably because <u>you're</u> much too indulgent with him. <u>Your</u> child-rearing methods are too relaxed. <u>You're</u> making a mistake if you think <u>your</u> devil-may-care approach to parenting will work. <u>Your</u> son doesn't respect you, and if this lack of discipline continues, <u>you're</u> going to wind up bailing him out of jail one day.

41. Answers will vary.

42. Answers will vary.

43. Answers will vary.

44. Answers will vary.

45. Answers will vary.

46. Answers will vary.

47. Answers will vary.

48. Answers will vary.

49. Answers will vary.

50. Answers will vary.

51. Answers will vary.

52. Answers will vary.

53. Answers will vary.

54. The rule is that lowercase letters are pronounced as they are in ordinary writing, but capital letters are pronounced as one would pronounce that letter while reciting it in the alphabet. The

six words written above are *hello*, *teacher*, *spelling, Mexico*, *happiness*, and *crazy*. Applying the rule to the other six words would produce PQlER, BhAVR, XprS, NtICng, sNTnL, and KtRR.

55. Answers may vary, but they will most likely be similar to the following:
I'm sorry. You can't come with us.
The butler stood by the door and called the guests names.
Look at that man-eating chicken.
A smart dog knows it's master.
Call me, fool, if you want.

56. The paragraph should read as follows: The spaces we put between words are essential for making sense of what we read. Without these spaces, our words become an **incomprehensible** jumble. With all the spaces in the wrong places, **ordinary** writing starts to look like something written in a foreign language.

57. Answers will vary.

58. Answers will vary.

59. Answers will vary. Some probable answers include:

DRUNK GETS NINE MONTHS IN VIOLIN CASE
The drunk is sentenced to nine months in jail as a result of a court case involving a violin.
The drunk is sentenced to spend nine months in a violin case.

FARMER BILL DIES IN HOUSE
A legislative bill that has to do with farmers failed to win approval in the House of Representatives.
A farmer named Bill died in a house.

IRAQI HEAD SEEKS ARMS
The leader of Iraq is trying to buy military armaments.
A disembodied head in Iraq is hoping to find some disembodied arms.

BRITISH LEFT WAFFLES ON FALKLAND ISLANDS
Left-leaning British citizens are inconsistent on their position regarding the Falkland Islands.
British citizens traveled to the Falkland Islands and left some waffles there.

MINERS REFUSE TO WORK AFTER DEATH
There was a death in a mine-shaft and the miners now refuse to work there.
Miners refuse to continue working after they die.

KILLER SENTENCED TO DIE FOR SECOND TIME IN TEN YEARS
A killer has received a death sentence from a judge for the second time in ten years.
A killer has received a sentence that condemns him to die twice in ten years.

60. Answers will vary.

61. Answers will vary.

62. Answers will vary.

63. Answers will vary.

64. Answers will vary.

65. Theo played <u>well</u> in the ballgame.
   The pie tasted <u>good</u> last night.
   Quentin did a <u>good</u> job redecorating.

I don't feel <u>well</u> today.

I don't feel <u>good</u> today. (Both are acceptable sentences.)

I wish I could sing as <u>well</u> as William.

66. Answers will vary.

67. Answers will vary, though one possible method of classification might be to divide words into those whose ending is pronounced "shun" and those whose ending is pronounced "yun."

68. Answers will vary.

69. Answers will vary.

70. Answers will vary.

71. The first rule places in brackets any consonant followed by an *h* and removes the *h*. The first sentence reads *They have thought about getting their flu shots before lunch*. The second rule places an accent above any vowel followed by an *s* and removes the *s*. The second sentence reads *The best musician has only his innate talents and a little luck*. The third rule replaces the letters *e* and *r* with an exclamation mark. The third sentence reads *The better they perform, the more the singer's voice will reverberate*. The fourth rule replaces the letter *g* with a number: 6 for a soft "g," as in *giant*, 9 for a hard "g," as in *good*, and 3 for a silent "g," as in *night*. The fourth sentence reads *The genius of the magic show got the guests up on their feet, applauding in delight.* The fifth rule inverts any vowel pairings. The fifth sentence reads *They lingered over their hearty meal for an hour.*

72. The five sentences should be rewritten as follows:

Five twoce, you should interrognine sometwo using only the fivemal techniques.

188

Do you twot people three be elevender and beten, or do you prefer asiten people?
I ofeleven wear a threethree, and I twoder why no two thinks it's grnine.
The caten's mnine showed grnine fivetithreede during the elevense wnine.
The debnine over five-enseven wasn't conducted with exactithreede.

73. Answers may vary, but the sentences should be rewritten roughly as follows:
When the black light dims, I open my eyes.
First year, the army retreated as near as the ugly valleys.
Before skipping away from the tunnel, they failed in losing an obscure disadvantage.
Her old-lost apathy for death was happily eternal.
Under the bottom of the ditch, she dropped her hand in compliance.

74. I am *so* furious at you!
Janet loves *The Lord of the Rings*.
Their apartment has really nice *gemutlichkeit*.

75. square meal, for instance, too funny for words, for once in my life, Robin Hood

76. The words that can be formed are *resist*, *relieve*, *retain*, *subsist*, *subordinate*, *exhale*, *exist*, *inhale*, *influence*, *insist*, *inordinate*, *confluence*, *consist*, *contain*, and *believe*.

77. The words that can be formed are *governor*, *government*, *governess*, *upper*, *upward*, *uppity*, *container*, *containment*, *backer*, *backward*, *kinder*, *kindly*, *kindness*, *validly*, and *validity*. It should be noted that the suffixes in *governess* and *kinder* function differently than they do in other instances of -*er* and -*ness* in this list.

78. Answers will vary.

79. Answers will vary.

80. Answers will vary.

81. Answers will vary. One possible set of solutions is as follows:
    Don't go.
    She ran quickly from the surprisingly aggressive squirrel.
    The painfully slow, boring, and idle wait finally came to a satisfyingly abrupt conclusion.
    Handsome John waited patiently.

82. <u>It's</u> all right, <u>it's</u> okay, you'll be working for us someday.
    The storm unleashed <u>its</u> fury right above our house.
    When all's said and done, <u>it's</u> better to be the one who leaves the relationship.
    The cat meowed <u>its</u> head off, as if to say, "<u>It's</u> time for my dinner!"

83. Answers will vary.

84. Answers will vary.

85. <u>Whether</u> the <u>weather</u> is cold, or <u>whether</u> the <u>weather</u> is hot, we'll be together whatever the <u>weather</u>, <u>whether</u> we like it or not.

86. Answers will vary.

87. How I long for a girl who understands what true romance is. All about you are sweet and faithful girls who are unlike you. Kiss the first boy who comes along, Adorabelle. I'd like to praise your beauty forever. I can't. Stop thinking you are the prettiest girl alive. Thine, Tyrone.

88. What did you come here for?
    He is the hottest guy I've ever laid eyes on.
    We have much to be thankful for.
    That depends on what you believe in.

89. Answers will vary.

90. Without vowels, it can be hard to follow what someone has written. Vowels occur commonly in written English. As you can see, it can be quite confusing without them!

91. Answers will vary.

92. Answers will vary.

93. Answers will vary.

94. Answers will vary.

95. Answers will vary. A complete list of punctuation marks should include the comma, period, question mark, exclamation mark, open quotes, closed quotes, apostrophe, colon, semicolon, dash, hyphen, ellipsis, open parentheses, and closed parentheses. A more adventurous list could include single quote marks as well as double quote marks, square brackets, rounded brackets, back slash, the em dash, and the en dash.

96. Answers will vary.

97. Answers will vary.

98. Some of the possible words follow. From *gr*: *gear*, *gore*, *eager*, *gyre*, *ogre*, and *gray*. From *str*: *stray*, *star*, *stair*, *stare*, *aster*, *store*, *steer*, and *satyr*. From *lt*: *late*, *lot*, *lit*, *lat*, *lute*, *alt*, and *loot*. From *sw*: *sway*, *saw*, *sew*, and *sow*. From *cd*: *cud*, *code*, *cod*, and *cede*.

99. Answers will vary.

100. Those people at SparkNotes sure are great.

101. Answers may vary. The sentences could be rewritten as follows:
    The actor, who weighed 200 pounds, was a tall man with a red moustache.
    The teacher posted the times discussed in class for the students.
    To get to work, Jimmy took the subway, definitely the most convenient method of travel.
    My mother told me that Maurice sent me flowers.
    Grandma Tina caught the martini glass that was sailing toward the floor.

102. I have <u>more</u> time to sleep on the weekends.
    I don't have <u>many</u> hours left before class.
    Zelda has <u>many</u> problems. However, Scott has even <u>more</u> problems than she does.
    Hal owns <u>more</u> records than Harry, but Harry has <u>more</u> MP3s.

103. There are at least eight possible pronunciations for the letters *ough* as exemplified in the following eight words: *thought*, *tough*, *though*, *through*, *cough*, *bough*, *Scarborough*, and *hiccough* (the British spelling of *hiccup*).

104. Answers may vary. The sentences could be rewritten as follows:
    Neither Jonas nor Marianne is coming tonight.
    Tonight's program could be either Bach or Beethoven.
    Houses can be built either from wood or from brick.

Neither Fox News nor CNN is unbiased.
Neither Gordon nor Sally likes Chinese food.

105. The blanks should be filled out the first time as *I, me, my*, and *mine*, and the second time as *Batman and I, Batman and me, Batman's and my*, and *Batman's and mine*. Going through the second time is just a matter of adding *Batman and* or *Batman's and* as appropriate.

106. Answers will vary.

107. Hector, an excellent judge, is always <u>disinterested</u>.
Helen is completely <u>uninterested</u> in dating Hector.
George and Martha called a trusted, <u>disinterested</u> friend to settle their dispute.
Far from being <u>disinterested</u>, Corzine welcomes bribes and is <u>uninterested</u> in fairness.
<u>Uninterested</u> in the circus, Garrett read a book as the clowns performed.

108. Answers will vary.

109. Answers may vary, but some common verb-preposition combinations include: *go off, go down, go out, run around, run off, run down, run up, run out, call off,call up, call out, give off, give up, give out, shoot off*, and *shoot up*.

110. Answers will vary.

111. Paragraphs will vary. *Buckle* can mean either "to put into place" (*Buckle your seat belts*) or "to collapse" (*The front end buckled*). *Left* can refer either to a departure (*They left by train*) or to remaining (*I'm the only person left*). *Oversight* can mean either "careful scrutiny" (*The factory thrives under his oversight*) or "failure to be observant" (*Her oversight cost the company thousands of dollars*). *Screen* can mean either "to show" (*We'll be screening my new film*

this evening) or "to conceal" (*If she hadn't screened the goaltender, the shot never would have gone in*).

112. Answers will vary.

113. Answers will vary.

114. Answers will vary.

115. Elinor had to choose <u>among</u> four suitors.
     Louis walked <u>between</u> the black and the red buildings.
     I felt at peace sitting <u>among</u> my five closest friends in the world.
     Greg strolled <u>amid</u> the trees all night.
     Jessie can never choose <u>between</u> the peach and mango sorbets.

116. Answers will vary.

117. Answers will vary.

118. A few of the possibilities: *drape, craps, grape, graph*; *bares, cares, caret, dares, eared, fares, hares, harem, pares, wares*; *blame, clams, clamp, flame, llama, slams*; *doses, hoses, loses, loser, mosey, noses, poses, poser, roses*

119. Answers will vary.

120. Answers will vary.

121. Answers will vary.

122. Answers may vary. The sentences could be rewritten as follows:
     Melissa's mom accused Melissa of being too fat.

Mike and Peter played baseball; Peter hit a home run.

When Janie and Melanie went to lunch, Janie confessed that she had kissed Hank the night before.

George told Simon that he, George, wanted to leave the party early.

123. There are two possible solutions for each sentence.

If they plan to attend the picnic, they each need to bring a few sandwiches.

If you plan to attend the picnic, you need to bring a few sandwiches.

When we were learning French, the most important thing we did was study grammar every day. When you learned French, the most important thing you did was study grammar every day.

If one is attending a dinner party, one should remember not to eat too much in the afternoon.

If you are attending a dinner party, you should remember not to eat too much in the afternoon.

124. Answers will vary.

125. Gail gave a really nice dictionary to George and me. (no rewrite necessary)

We girls love to go out dancing.

Claire and he got in a huge fight last night.

Are Eduardo and she coming to dinner later?

126. Answers will vary.

127. Answers will vary.

128. The two possible sentences are: *Wherever you tan, do utter, 'rest, trials goad amateur chins,'* and *Where very out-and-out terrestrials go, Adam ate urchins.*

129. Answers will vary.

130. less alcohol; less bread; fewer cars; less oxygen; fewer particles; fewer seeds; fewer spaceships; fewer spoons; less sugar; less water

131. Answers will vary.

132. Answers will vary.

133. Answers will vary.

134. Answers may vary. The sentences could be rewritten as follows:
Remember never to split an infinitive.
Never use the passive voice.
Place pronouns as close to their antecedents as possible, especially in long sentences, as of ten or more words.
If any word is, a linking verb is improper at the end of a sentence.
Everyone should be careful to use a singular pronoun with singular nouns in his or her writing.

135. *Opticals* means "glasses," *eartops* means "earrings," *blur* means "confused" or "ignorant," *baas* means "boss," *barney* means "fight," *gas* means "ridiculous" or "funny," *tuque* means "wool hat," and *hard* means "blunt" or "obnoxious."

136. Answers will vary.

137. Everyone should be allowed to sleep whenever he or she wants, but I draw the line at going to bed at three in the afternoon. My boyfriend, Gabe, refuses to go to sleep at a normal time: he insists on staying awake until he passes out from exhaustion. His mother doesn't care, but I can't stand going out with a guy with such an irregular schedule.

138. After all, what is this film but a collection of car chases?
Victor asked me what I was doing later.
I wondered how you're coping with your mother's illness. (no rewrite necessary)
Why did Preston come here, if all he planned to do was whine and complain?

139. Answers will vary.

140. My dad took me to see *Gladiator* at Union Square.
Andrew's favorite episode of the TV show *Fawlty Towers* is called "The Kipper and the Corpse."
Lila always listens to the Beatles' song "I'm Still Sleeping," which is on the album *Revolver*.
I read a really interesting article in the *New York Times Magazine* called "Fixing Nemo."

141. Answers will vary.

142. Answers will vary.

143. Answers will vary.

144. Answers will vary.

145. Answers will vary. According to this exercise, the "opposite" of progress is Congress.

146. Jake's the loveliest guy I've ever met.
I won't go to the party unless you come with me.
We're happy to see you.
I can't believe how fat that cat has gotten.
Jean hadn't prepared for Alice's departure.
You shouldn't stay out all night before an exam.

Andrew didn't stay long at the restaurant.
I haven't had time to study.

147. Answers will vary.

148. Answers will vary. The following twenty-five words include silent letters in alphabetical order (skipping *v*): *marriage*, *doubt*, *indict*, *handkerchief*, *love*, *halfpenny*, *night*, *fight*, *business*, *rijsttafel*, *know*, *salmon*, *mnemonic*, *autumn*, *laboratory*, *psychotic*, *racquet*, *forecastle*, *island*, *ballet*, *gauge*, *wrong*, *faux*, *crayon*, *rendezvous*.

149. Answers will vary. *Defenselessness* is one of the longest words with only one vowel.

150. Answers will vary. The longest common words that can be typed using only the left hand include *reverberates*, *desegregated*, and *stewardesses*. The longest common word that can be typed using only the right hand is *homophony*.

151. The code is as follows: A = Q, B = W, C = E, D = R, E = M, F = T, G = Y, H = U, I = O, J = I, K = P, L = A, M = S, N = D, O = F, P = G, Q = H, R = J, S = K, T = L, U = Z, V = X, W = C, X = V, Y = B, Z = N. The paragraph, decoded, reads: **The best way to** crack a code is to start with a few familiar elements. Take a few guesses about **the letters** that come up quite often, and from those guesses, see if you can piece together a few of the words. Slowly but surely, you'll work out the meanings of more and more letters. It **may be** slow going at first, but as you make inroads it will become easier and easier.

152. Answers will vary.

153. Answers will vary.

154. Answers will vary.

155. *Independence*, *embarrassment*, *ecstasy*, *millennium*, and *judgment* are spelled correctly. The other five italicized words should be spelled *adolescence*, *definitely*, *repetition*, *existence*, and *minuscule*.

156. The speaker the students heard yesterday <u>was</u> one of the congressmen from Wisconsin.
Neither the judge nor the jury <u>is</u> at fault.
Even though the effects of eating french fries <u>are</u> well known, many people can't resist the greasy treat.
Next to the perfume aisle, on top of a forgotten shelf, <u>sits</u> a dusty mitten.

157. Answers will vary.

158. Answers will vary.

159. Answers will vary.

160. Answers may vary. The paragraph could be rewritten as follows:
We decided to go to Italy and chose Capri as our destination. John, who loves swimming, had always wanted to swim in the ocean around Capri. There was a huge rainstorm the night before we reached our hotel, so when we arrived the streets were still wet. John wanted to visit the Blue Grotto right away, but I wanted to unpack. I was changing into my swimsuit when a goat walked right into our room!

161. Answers will vary. Some examples of words containing four consecutive letters are *understudy*, *overstuff*, and *gymnoplast*.

162. Answers will vary.

163. If you think Sharon's smart, <u>then</u> you're insane.
Geraldine arrived, <u>then</u> Allan showed up.

I ate breakfast; <u>then</u> I went for a run.

I would rather eat breakfast <u>than</u> go running.

164. Answers will vary.

165. Answers will vary.

166. Answers will vary.

167. Answers will vary. Three possible answers for each scrambled sentence:

The light shines brightly over the blue room.; The blue light shines brightly over the room.; The brightly blue light shines over the room.

The old man gave the whistle to his grandson.; The grandson gave the whistle to his old man.; The man gave his old whistle to the grandson.

I'm going to meet my best friend in New York.; I'm going to meet my new best friend in New York.; I'm in New York, going to meet my best friend.

Wind the clock before it gets late.; Clock the wind before it gets late.; Before the clock gets late, wind it.

When you get here, say what you did.; When did you say what you get here?; Did you say when you get what here?

168. Answers will vary.

169. Answers will vary. One possible set of answers:

Each of the cars in that lot <u>has</u> a red stripe across the hood.

Everybody in the concert hall <u>is</u> wearing a suit.

Each and every student <u>is</u> responsible for <u>his or her</u> own actions.

Everyone in the café <u>is</u> unhappy with <u>his or her</u> dinner.

170. Answers will vary.

171. E-is there enough time to drop by my house on the way?
She i-is the youngest person ever to win a gold medal in archery.
Andy, the new team captain, p-is really responsible.

172. Answers will vary. One possible set of solutions:
You seem concerned and hurt. You might not think that I care. I do.
I think that I might not hurt you. You care and do seem concerned.
I think you might hurt and I do care that you not seem concerned.

173. Answers will vary. One possible set of solutions:
Why she should want to know how it's done is beyond me.
I wonder where I would be now if I'd known how to do what I was told.
What I don't know is how you got to where you were going when there was so much snow on the ground.
Asking who did what to whom isn't important when there's no explanation of why the keys aren't where I put them.
If you are who you say you are, you'll know why I mean what I mean when I ask how you got to where the money is hidden.

174. The four letters, from top to bottom and left to right, are o, n, a, and m.

175. Answers will vary.

176. Answers will vary.

177. The computer that that Charlie bought is green.
The computer, which comes in green, blue, and silver, appeals to children.
I dislike editorials that express racist opinions.
The editorial expressing racist opinions, which appeared in the student newspaper, angered everyone.
He wrote a book that debunked the glamour of Marilyn Monroe.

178. The person who hit my car should have to pay to fix the damages.
The people who have been standing in line the longest should get in first.
Give the movie tickets to whomever you like.
Give the movie tickets to whoever seems to want them most.

179. Answers will vary.

180. Answers may vary. The sentences could be rewritten as follows:
Nobody can stop me from dreaming.
Joe can't wait for gym class.
Joe can hardly wait for gym class.
It's impossible not to scream when you watch this movie. (no correction needed)
There isn't any way to get a perfect score.
There is no way to get a perfect score.
If Mama isn't happy, nobody is happy.